HISTORY OF
TRAINS

Massimo Ferrari · Emanuele Lazzati

HISTORY OF TRAINS

CRESCENT BOOKS
New York

Additional material by Basil Cooper

Translated by John Gilbert

This 1990 edition published by
Crescent Books, distributed by Outlet Book
Company, Inc.,
a Random House Company,
225 Park Avenue South,
New York, New York 10003

ISBN 0-517-03315-1

8 7 6 5 4 3 2 1

The publishers wish to thank Ing. Piero
Muscolino, Direzione Centrale Relazioni
Estere, Ferrovie dello Stato, Rome

Typeset in Great Britain by Tradespools Ltd,
Frome, Somerset

Printed and bound in Italy

Frontispiece: A two-level train of the
Burlington Northern, designed for commuter
service in the suburbs of Chicago. During the
1950s the principal North American cities,
worshipping the cult of the automobile,
abandoned the majority of these rail services,
only to regret the decision when later faced
with the increasingly insurmountable problem
of road traffic congestion. Nowadays
commuter services of this kind operate only in
Boston, New York, Philadelphia, Chicago,
San Francisco, Montreal and Toronto.

Opposite: Front view of the Pendolino,
designed for fast connections between Milan
and Rome, thanks to the angle of inclination
of the train body to the rails, enabling curves
to be negotiated at speeds of over 30 per cent
higher than that of traditional trains. Recently
the routes of the Pendolino have also been
extended to Naples, Turin and Venice.

On page 6: A spectacular night-time view of
the station of Montparnasse in Paris, the
departure point for direct trains to Normandy
and Brittany.

CONTENTS

PREFACE 7

CH. 1 • FROM STEPHENSON TO THE TGV 8
The dawn of a new age 10
Railway mania 12
Mountain railways 19
The golden age of the wagons-lits 20
The climactic years 30
The railways in wartime 39
The great crisis 42
A phoenix rises again 44

Ch. 2 • TRAINS IN ART AND LITERATURE 46
The "monster" in literature 48
Railway architecture 53
The rhythm of the train 58
The image of speed 62
The screen version 66

Ch. 3 • WAR AND PEACE 74
A new way of going to war 76
The carriage at Compiègne 83
The train as last bastion of empire 85
The nemesis of history – violence and the train 86
Pacts and agreements 88

Ch. 4 • THE GREAT TRAINS 90
The Flying Scotsman 94
Intercity 125 96
Lapplandspilen 100
Mistral 102
Glacier Express 103
Treno del Sole 104
Carlo Magno and Leonardo da Vinci 106
Andalus Expreso 108
Chopin 112

Rossia 114
Taurus Express 115
Himalayan Queen 116
North Star 118
Reunification Train 119
Canadian 121
Panama Limited 124
Aguila Azteca 125
Tren de Sierra 126
Lagos del Sur 128
Ghan 129
Blue Train 130

Ch. 5 • A TRAIN FOR ALL SEASONS 134
The train as liberator 136
The train to town 138
Private and nationalized services 142
Exotic, tropical and arctic trains 144
Train links with sea and air 145
Underground and city trains 148
Hill and mountain trains 153
Trains of dreams and regrets 156

Ch. 6 • THE FUTURE OF THE RAILWAYS 164
Europe 166
North America 168
Latin America 172
The Soviet Union 174
Japan 177
India 180
China 183
Africa 186
Australia 188

PICTURE SOURCES 190

BIBLIOGRAPHY 191

PREFACE

This is not a history of the railways, nor is it a technical work, but a collection of our personal observations, anecdotes and jottings, based on our boundless passion for rail travel.

In spite of the many technological advances that may in some ways be argued to have almost superseded it, the train is still very much alive and well. There is much enthusiasm and interest in the glorious and valuable part it still plays in our industrial civilization. Long may this continue.

The authors

CHAPTER 1

FROM STEPHENSON TO THE TGV

"Those who did not know France before the Revolution cannot understand the meaning of the sweetness of living." The author of these words, the Prince de Talleyrand, was certainly a reactionary, but one of great vision. A former priest and diplomat who engineered the restoration of the monarchy at the Congress of Vienna, Tallyrand realized that, appearances notwithstanding, the past would never return and that an age had ended forever. The sweetness of life which he mourned was now a memory cherished only by a privileged few. The mass culture which was evolving in the wake of the Revolution would henceforth be directed towards technical and productive development, with all the attendant marvels and horrors that this would entail for generations to come.

There is no telling whether Talleyrand, as he approached his death in 1838, could have foreseen the further revolution that was already underway, imposed not by Napoleonic bayonets but following the advent of the steam engine. Here was a revolution that would not be strangled by the guardians of authority. Nor is it likely that such far-reaching implications occurred to those gentlemen who had gathered 13 years earlier in a field in Darlington, England, to watch the first steam locomotive to provide a public transport service go puffing on its way. For it was England that pioneered the iron monster which was soon to emerge as the very symbol of progress throughout the world.

As is the case with all the great inventions which have transformed human life, the story of trains and railways is littered with dates, both glorious and inglorious alike. Some books list these in strict chronological order. We have tried, instead, to evoke certain significant moments in this long journey. At present France is inheriting the mantle of Stephenson, builder of the first locomotive to work on a public railway, demonstrating, with the TGV (Train à Grande Vitesse) that the marvel of rail travel is still alive but perhaps there will come a time when the steam engine will be no more than a museum piece and the railway as we know it a relic of the past.

THE DAWN OF A NEW AGE

The years 1813–18, highlighted by the Battle of the Nations (Leipzig), Waterloo and the Congress of Vienna, were important for the conception of the self-propelled wheel which, as it moved, generated inertial force, for William Hedley's "Puffing Billy," the first locomotive with more than one driving axle, to be used in the Wylam colliery in Northumberland. George Stephenson would subsequently improve and perfect the "Puffing Billy."

The revolutionary application of a piston rod, moved by the compression of steam and connected to the driving wheels, paved the way for events of that famous day of Tuesday 27 September 1825, when locomotive no. 1, Locomotion, preceded by the builder himself, triumphantly hauled a train for a distance of 24 miles (39 km) from the mining town of Darlington to the river banks of Stockton-on-Tees.

The train was made up of six coal wagons and six bags of grain, a covered compartment for officials and notables, and 21 carriages with 588 passengers seated on wooden planks. The total weight was 70 tonnes and the train travelled at an average speed of 6 mph (10 kmh), with 20 stops.

It was almost inevitable that this development should take place in the North of England, then, arguably, one of the wealthiest areas in the world with the highest concentration of industry and population density, the cities being situated at no great distance from one another (the Manchester–Liverpool rail connection and, in Scotland, the Glasgow–Edinburgh line would soon follow).

The internal combustion engine, which made possible the invention of the automobile and the airplane, and which burst on

Opposite: George Stephenson's Rocket locomotive, pictured outside London's Royal Albert Hall in August 1979, will go down in history as the first passenger train engine, which covered the 24-mile (39-km) distance from Darlington to Stockton-on-Tees in the North of England on 27 September 1825, giving rise to a veritable revolution in transport and communications. Today it is exhibited to the public in the National Railway Museum, York, England.

Below: The plan for another early locomotive by the engineer George Trevithick, for use in coal-mines.

On the previous page: A TGV speeds through the French countryside, the almost unrecognizable descendant of the early puffing monsters of the nineteenth century.

TREVITHICKS,
PORTABLE STEAM ENGINE.

Catch me who can.

Mechanical Power Subduing Animal Speed.

the world like an exploding firework, was the culmination of diverse ideas and experiments, in various countries; the concept of steam as a source of energy, however, was the brainchild of just one man, and in due course its application for industrial purposes would occur in England. In 1827, Restoration France was to launch the country's first railway line, running from the coal-mining area of Saint-Etienne, already an important industrial center, to Andrezieux on the Loire. The birth of rail can thus be seen to be directly linked to mining.

In 1827 the Austro-Hungarian empire would in its turn inaugurate a rail link between Vienna and Wagram, and in 1830 the first North American steam engine, the Best Friend, made its appearance in Charleston. The nineteenth-century battles for control of the railways would involve wealthy and powerful families such as the Goulds, Drews and Vanderbilts, formidable orchestrators of mammoth financial deals on the floor of New York's Stock Exchange.

Among the most influential European families were the Rothschilds in France, the oldest and perhaps the most famous branch of that legendary dynasty of bankers and philanthropists, which had built up its fortunes prior to the introduction of the railways through fortunate speculation on the stock exchange, thanks to its carrier pigeon service between Brussels and Paris, which brought advance information of the battle of Waterloo, in a way the earliest instance of market-rigging.

Many countries were quick to recognize the advantages of the railways, and to translate their enthusiasm into financial investment. The Societé Générale de Belgique, for example, created by the

House of Orange, rulers of the Netherlands, invested in railways throughout the world as early as 1822.

Great Britain also envisaged far-reaching benefits in the applications of the railways in her overseas empire. The Indian subcontinent was thus provided with a comprehensive railway system, at its inception mainly military in purpose, which afforded the most convenient means of transporting colonial troops, after the rising of 1857, to every strategic corner of that vast country.

Indeed, Great Britain was to emerge as one of the leading nineteenth-century nations, and the railways were greatly instrumental in bringing this about. While many often expressed dislike and even contempt for these technical and scientific innovations, the tide of progress was, inevitably, unstoppable.

RAILWAY MANIA

Queen Victoria came to the throne in 1837, when London's main-line terminals had not yet been planned (including the station which would later be dedicated to her and bear her name). In a reign of more than 60 years she would live to see the steady growth and consolidation of railway networks all over the world.

In 1831 Belgium obtained her independence from the Netherlands, thus paving the way for a plan, devised by King Leopold I, which would achieve the double purpose of amalgamating Walloons and Flemings into a single nation and raising the status of the port of Antwerp, from which the first colonists would soon depart for Africa and the East Indies. This led to the notion of linking the country's main towns by rail, the first 15 miles (25 km) of such a

12

Steam traction remained unchallenged throughout the nineteenth century.
Below: One of the earliest trains from the first half of the nineteenth century.
Opposite: Detail of one of the most recent locomotives of the Ferrovie Nord, Milan, Italy. The elegance of the lines and the finish clearly illustrates the considerable development that has taken place in railway design over a period of just a few decades.

network, from Brussels to Malines, being opened by the king on 5 May 1835.

Seven months later, on 7 December 1835, the first stretch of railway in Germany – a mere 4 miles (6 km) from Nuremberg to Fürth – was opened, named Ludwigsbahn in honour of King Ludwig I of Bavaria. A solemn Orthodox ceremony – complete with tolling bells, priests chanting hymns and sprinkling holy water, and magnificently resonant choirs – marked the opening on 30 October 1837 of the first Russian railway line from St Petersburg to Pavlovsk, towards the imperial summer residence of the Tsar of all the Russias, Nicholas I, who would later persuade Metternich to embark on the Warsaw–Vienna railway, completed in the fateful

revolutionary year of 1848. Within ten years there was to be a line open to Moscow, with a double track running through swamp and marshland, its 4 ft 11 in (1,524 mm) gauge remaining the standard for that immense country. The construction of this railway involved an army of serfs who were subjected to long and harsh working hours, frequently flogged, and decimated by swamp fever and venereal disease.

A London station now long forgotten was the scene of a royal occasion on 7 March 1856. This was Bricklayers Arms, a terminus built jointly by the London, Brighton and South Coast and the South Eastern Railways to avoid the tolls imposed by the Greenwich Railway for using their line into the terminus at London Bridge. Bricklayers Arms was gaily decorated to greet Princess Alexandra of Denmark when she arrived by special train from Gravesend for her marriage to the Prince of Wales.

In later years complete royal trains were built to supplement the individual saloons. The London, Brighton and South Coast Railway boasted "a stately five-coach, all-clerestoried set in shining mahogany and gilt lining out, headed by an engine which always had a magnificent casting of the Royal Arms in the full glory of heraldic colours on the front." The description comes from a dim childhood memory of an observer who saw this splendid cavalcade at Epsom Downs station on Derby Day, towering above the assortment of nondescript steam engines and rackety suburban coaches which had brought the public to the race meeting.

Queen Victoria died in January 1901 on the Isle of Wight. A hitch in the arrangements delayed the funeral train, conveying crowned heads and other dignitaries of

Church and State, and it was essential to make up time on the journey from Gosport to London so that the timetable for the procession in London could be observed. Urged to do his best, the driver created a railway legend by attaining an estimated speed of 92 mph (148 kmh) as the train raced down a gradient near Dorking in Surrey. Like other speed achievements in the early years of the century, however, sceptics have disputed the maximum speed and put it nearer to 75 mph (120.7 kmh), the severe curves at this point having probably exaggerated the impression of speed. A railway official who travelled in the saloon recalled in later years having put out his hand to steady the coffin when it seemed in danger of falling off the trestles on which it was supported. Whatever the maximum speed may have been, the train arrived at Victoria station two minutes early and earned the driver the congratulations of the German Emperor.

In the 1840s a man emerged in the field of railway building whose dominant personality earned him the title of "The Railway King." He was George Hudson, who had begun his working life in a draper's shop in York, Northern England, but by 1837 had risen to become Lord Mayor of the city. A legacy of £30,000 enabled him to enter the world of business where he showed outstanding acumen and enterprise. In later years, when he had overreached himself, he looked back to his inheritance as the first step to disaster.

Hudson was elected chairman of the newly formed York and North Midland Railway in 1839. This line connected the city of York with other railways to the South of England serving Leeds and London. A year later he leased the Leeds and Selby Railway but promptly shut most of it

For a long time Great Britain rightly regarded itself as representing the avant-garde in railway engineering. *Opposite:* The famous Cock o' the North, an advanced locomotive of the London and North Eastern Railway, also tested for experimental runs in France, here seen in the workshops at Doncaster with its coachwork partially removed to facilitate overhaul. *Below:* A curious project designed literally to harness horse power to rail. After Stephenson's success many years passed before the railway network in Great Britain took on its present guise. There were heated debates as to which gauge should be adopted. Eventually a special commission, including experts on astronomy and mathematics, recommended a 4 ft 8 in (1,435 mm) measurement, already chosen by Stephenson for his first train.

to passenger traffic so that travellers would be obliged to follow a more roundabout route using the York and North Midland line.

The hectic period known as "The Railway Mania" had now begun. Hundreds of schemes were promoted and money poured in from all sides from shareholders hoping to profit quickly from the new means of transport. Only a few were approved by Parliament. Some were completely fraudulent. They would attract money by issuing impressive prospectuses headed by the names of well-known public figures without their consent.

Hudson kept his head in these tumultuous times. His main concern was to establish a railway system serving the important industrial towns in the Midlands and to create a route to Scotland through Northeast England. This was being done on the

West Coast by the London and North Western Railway and its associates. The London terminus of the LNWR at Euston had become known as "The Gateway to the North" and at first all trains to the North of England and Scotland had to travel over LNWR tracks between London and Rugby. Hudson accepted this situation and concentrated on the northern territories. His major coup was the founding of the Midland Railway in 1844 by amalgamating three separate companies radiating from Derby which brought Leicester, Nottingham and Birmingham into his empire. He still did not have his own line to London, and by the time the Midland Railway reached London at St Pancras station in 1868 his power had waned.

In Hudson's northern domain the Great North of Scotland Railway connected York with Darlington in 1841. Further construction by Hudson companies brought the railway to Berwick-on-Tweed by 1847. He was also involved in the construction of the North British Railway between Berwick and Edinburgh. The opening of the Royal Border Bridge completed a continuous rail link under Hudson control from Rugby to Scotland.

Hudson always opposed the building of a railway from London to York. In the end he was overruled when the Great Northern Railway was created by an Act of 1846, entitling it to build a line from London to the village of Askern, north of Doncaster. It was often said that the Great Northern Railway "ended in a field," but this was where it joined a branch of the Lancashire and Yorkshire Railway, over which its trains reached York. This route was opened in 1850 and in 1857 was joined at Hitchin by a branch from Leicester over

The prototype of the high-speed ETR 500 electric train. Thanks to this train, Italy became one of the European countries equipped with railway services capable of linking its principal cities at average speeds of 155 mph (250 kmh). If present work goes according to plan it should be possible, by the end of the century, to travel from Milan to Rome in 3 hours, from Rome to Munich in 5 hours and

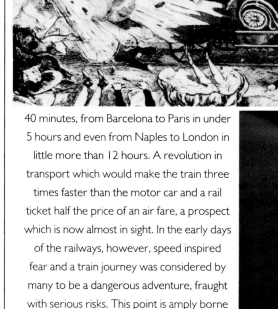

40 minutes, from Barcelona to Paris in under 5 hours and even from Naples to London in little more than 12 hours. A revolution in transport which would make the train three times faster than the motor car and a rail ticket half the price of an air fare, a prospect which is now almost in sight. In the early days of the railways, however, speed inspired fear and a train journey was considered by many to be a dangerous adventure, fraught with serious risks. This point is amply borne out by the etching (above) by H. Hughes, ironically entitled *The Joys of the Railway* (1831).

which Midland trains travelled to London until their own terminus at St Pancras was opened in 1868.

With the opening of the Great Northern Railway from London to York the East Coast Route to Scotland was complete, apart from the completion of a shorter route from Doncaster to Peterborough. By this time Hudson had left the scene. Share prices tumbled after the Railway Mania, and anxious shareholders began to question some of Hudson's financial dealings. It was found that he had been keeping the shares of his companies artificially high by paying dividends out of capital, and had concealed the sale of shares from the companies' books so that he could keep the money himself. At a meeting of the Eastern Counties Railway in 1849 feelings against him were so strong that he was hissed and booed. Soon afterwards he resigned the chairmanship of the Midland Railway. He had gone into obscurity by the time the East Coast Route, to which he had contributed so much, was completed, and by the time the Midland reached London he was a forgotten force. The North Eastern Railway conducted a long lawsuit against him to recover debts to the company and in 1865 he was sent to prison in York for three months as a debtor. He died in 1871.

When Hudson's Midland Railway at last reached London the railway map of Britain seemed to be complete. But there were many forceful personalities in nineteenth-century railway management, and one of them was to promote the building of Britain's last main line. He was Edward Watkin, who first came into prominence when, as secretary of the Trent Valley Railway Company, he negotiated a successful deal with the London and North Western Railway whereby the North Western acquired

Below: A nineteenth-century print shows the bridge over the Venetian lagoon, built in 1846. One of the first great railway enterprises, it brought profound changes to the habits of those living in one of the most famous cities in the world.

Opposite: Giuseppe Verdi as a young man. The great composer visited St Petersburg in the winter of 1861–2, by invitation of Tsar Alexander II, to attend the première of *La Forza del Destino*. To reach the Russian city, he had to make a long train journey from Italy via Paris and Berlin.

the Trent Valley line and so had a direct route from Rugby to Stafford. Trains for points north of Stafford no longer had to travel via Birmingham, which shortened distances and diverted traffic from an area already working to capacity.

Watkin worked for a time with the North Western at Euston and then climbed rapidly in the railway hierarchy, becoming chairman in 1864 of the Manchester, Sheffield and Lincolnshire Railway. This was a struggling cross-country company, carrying a heavy freight traffic but having to hand over much of it to other railways for transport to London and the South. From Sheffield its lines penetrated into Nottinghamshire where many collieries were served. Watkin was also Chairman of the Metropolitan Railway, which was extending northwards through suburban London

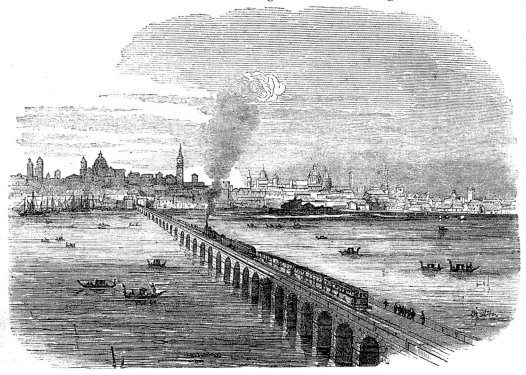

to rural Buckinghamshire. Looking at his properties in the Midlands and the Home Counties, Watkin planned to connect them by building a new line, 92 miles (147 km) long, through Nottingham, Leicester and Rugby to join the Metropolitan at a point north of Aylesbury.

Watkin's plan was bitterly opposed by the other railways but in 1893 the Manchester, Sheffield and Lincolnshire Railway was granted an Act authorizing it to build a new line which would give it its own access to London. In 1897 the company changed its name to Great Central, and in March 1899 it began regular services between its Marylebone terminus in London and the Midlands and North. Its trains were in competition at all important towns along the route with the services of the older companies, but the railway concentrated on building a "new image" with fast trains and buffet cars on all long-distance services. The rival lines had tended to become complacent and buffet or restaurant cars were provided only on the most prestigious trains. The new rival stimulated competition and the travelling public as a whole benefited. But it was a hard struggle for the Great Central and it was just getting on its feet when the First World War broke out and all railways came under Government control. Dividends on its shares had always been meager or nonexistent and when it was operating under its old name critics claimed that the initials MSL stood for money sunk and lost. When the change in name was made the new initials were interpreted as standing for "Gone Completely."

Watkin's somewhat grandiose plans for the railway were stopped by the war. Among his chairmanships was that of the South Eastern Railway whose main line ran

from London to Dover. This line could be linked with the Metropolitan. Watkin was therefore in control of a continuous railway route from Manchester to the English Channel. As chairman of the first Channel Tunnel Company, Watkin dreamed of through trains between Manchester and Paris. Plans for a Channel Tunnel had been dropped by the time of his death in 1875 but a century later the project was revived and after some false starts work on the tunnel began in earnest in 1988. Through trains between Manchester and Paris could become a reality but they will not follow Watkin's Great Central line. In the period of rationalization after the Second World War the Great Central was seen all too obviously as duplicating other routes. It was the first British main line to be closed.

MOUNTAIN RAILWAYS

As a result of joint German, Swiss and Italian proposals, on 1 November 1871 the Compagnia Ferroviaria del Gottardo was set up in Lucerne, and in less than 20 years the Gotthard Tunnel was completed. With its Swiss, German and Italian backers the Gotthard line was the first international railway enterprise. Over the centuries the rivers Rhine, Rhône and Reuss had carved a natural highway from north to south, crossing the mountains by the St Gotthard Pass and dropping down the valley of the Tessin. For years trade followed this route.

The Gotthard Tunnel beween Göschenen and Airolo is 9.3 miles (15 km) long. It has always been double-track but there were single-track sections on the approaches until 1893. Seven spiral tunnels as the line climbs to the summit restrict the gradient for the most part to 1 in 38.5 by increasing the distance in which the change in level has to be accomplished. The highest point is at an altitude of 3,776 ft (1,151 m). A traveller has recalled being surprised at seeing apparently three railways in the valley until he realized that he had just traversed the section of line below and would shortly be entering on the one above. The little church near the line at Wassen is well known because the traveller sees it first on the left, then on the right, and finally on the right again as the train winds its way up the steep sides of the valley. At first the railway company provided observation cars from which passengers could have an unobstructed view of the magnificent scenery but these proved not to be a success. Being four-wheeled vehicles, the ride was bumpy and the open viewing platforms gave little protection from smoke and smuts. All trains stopped at Göschenen at the north end of the tunnel for the passengers to partake of refreshments at the station buffet. In later years, a *train de luxe* with a restaurant car was introduced and named the Gotthard Express. The journey from Lucerne to the Italian frontier at Chiasso took 5 hours 55 minutes with seven stops en route.

At the beginning of the twentieth century the Gotthard was supplemented by the Tauern Tunnel between Salzburg and Villach and the Karawanken, from Villach to Ljubljana – two Austro-Hungarian projects which provided the ideal means of linking central Europe with the Balkan peninsula.

Opened in May 1906, at the height of the Belle Epoque, an age of great material prosperity (if only for a few) and economic expansion, the Simplon Tunnel was hailed as a message of peace and concord among the peoples of Europe.

After the construction of the great international mountain tunnels, it was the turn of the hardly less important internal railways in the individual alpine states.

Below: Workers engaged in completing the Albula Tunnel, designed to link the Engadine with the rest of the Grisons canton and Switzerland as a whole. Thanks to this daring 1-m gauge railway, a region that was originally almost inaccessible would soon become the goal of holiday-makers. The fame of St Moritz as a resort is almost wholly due to this much-frequented line.

Opposite: A spectacular photograph of a Rhaetian Railways train approaching the winding series of tunnels which, extending for several kilometers, lead to the Rhine valley.

The remarkable Semmering line in Austria, however, opened in 1854 is generally acknowledged to have been the first railway to cross a mountain.

THE GOLDEN AGE OF THE WAGONS-LITS

Thanks to European inventiveness and technical prowess, which brought about the double miracle of the Fréjus Tunnel and the Suez Canal, the railways entered an expansionist phase as trains began to play a predominant role in national economies. With a view to countering the French-Italian partnership, the Germans focused their attention on plans for a Middle East line running from Berlin to Istanbul and Baghdad. The alliance with the declining Ottoman Empire was to endure until the outbreak of the Great War, eventually posing a threat to British dominion on the Indian subcontinent. This was also the period of a series of German archaeological discoveries, from Troy to Nineveh, made possible by economic penetration of the territories under Turkish authority.

In the meantime the European railway scene was transformed by the Belgian financier Georges Nagelmackers, enjoying the patronage of King Leopold II, the monarch who established Belgian colonial dominion over the Congo. Nagelmackers had been impressed by the ideas of George Mortimer Pullman, the Chicago-born American whose name introduced a new word into railway vocabulary. Nagelmackers was responsible for launching, in 1876, the Compagnie Internationale des Wagons-Lits, which in 1883 was given the additional description "et des Grands Express Européens"; the principal share-

holder, obviously, was Leopold II himself. "Pullman" is often thought to be synonymous with luxury but in fact the early cars were modest.

In the United States, a country of long distances, many journeys were made overnight. As early as 1836 the Cumberland Valley Railroad in Pennsylvania converted an ordinary coach to operate as a sleeping car between Harrisburg and Chambersburg. The vehicle was divided into four compartments, each with three bunks, one above the other, on one side of the car. Lighting was by candles, and a stove to burn coal or wood provided warmth in winter. Passengers lay down in their clothes on rough mattresses but there was a concession to comfort in the washbasin, water and a towel at one end of the car.

Other railways developed similar vehicles over the next two decades, offering various improvements such as the provision of sheets and blankets to which passengers helped themselves from a cupboard in the car. At a period when a night journey in France meant sitting up all night, a French visitor to the United States in 1848 was impressed by the cars he saw operating between Atlanta and Augusta (Georgia). In these vehicles there were four compartments, one or two reserved for

women, with three berths a side in each. During the day the two lower bunks formed a comfortable sofa. At night the back of the sofa was lowered to form the middle berth.

George Pullman thought he could improve on the efforts of contemporaries. In the early 1850s he persuaded the Chicago and Alton Railroad to let him convert two coaches according to his ideas. This was the origin of the sleeping car "section" for which Pullman took out a patent. A section consisted of one upper and one lower berth. The lower berth was formed by two seats facing each other. At night the backs were folded down and the seats were moved together to make a bed. At the same time the upper berth, which had been folded against the ceiling, was lowered by an arrangement of ropes and pulleys. There were four such sections on each side of the car.

Apart from these improvements in design, an important achievement by Pullman was his success in persuading different railway companies to include his cars in their trains and pass them on from one train to another where two lines connected. Previously passengers had been obliged to change at these points, often in the small hours, and join in the general stampede to find seats. Ten different companies were involved in providing continuous communication from Albany to Buffalo, and although a time of 14 hours was advertised for the journey of 290 miles (464 km), it could take much longer before the introduction of through carriages because of poor connections. Railway companies had been unwilling to allow their coaches to run over other companies' lines in case they were not returned, but Pullman's coaches were his own property and if he was prepared to send them on long through journeys there was no objection. Pullman

Opposite: A rare photograph of one of the first models of the Orient Express, undergoing a routine brake check. The opening of the great mountain tunnels at the end of the nineteenth century made rail links possible between northern Europe and the Mediterranean. At first, however, long train journeys were restricted to a small group of travellers, such as diplomats on their way to new postings, businessmen looking for favourable commercial deals and aristocrats in pursuit of leisure and literary dreams. It was the start of the Belle Epoque, which would also see the development of the alpine railways towards the newly established mountain resorts, as shown by the pictures on the right and below.

paid the railways for conveying his cars and earned revenue by collecting a supplement from the passengers who used them.

Well before the inception of the Common Market, Nagelmackers' initiative was, if not a precursor of continental unification, at least a practical first step towards the free and unimpeded crossing of national frontiers. Nagelmackers bears the credit for inaugurating the earliest direct link between Paris and Berlin via Brussels (the future Etoile du Nord), delayed as a result of the outbreak of the Franco-Prussian war of 1870. But in its stead the line was opened from Ostend to Brindisi, via Strasbourg (then German), Munich, Verona and the Adriatic coast.

Diplomatic mail would be loaded at

4. — Vallée de Conches (Valais).

Vue générale des travaux à Grengiols.

Chemin de fer Viège Zermatt près Stalden
3353 EDITION BURDE LITH. SAINT-IMIER

Bahn Visp-Zermatt bei Stalden

Brindisi and carried by sea to Bombay through the newly opened Suez Canal. The train, later converted for the passage through the Fréjus Tunnel, was subsequently known as the Peninsular Express, in recognition of the fact that most of the journey occurred on Italian soil.

Nagelmackers' company provided restaurant cars as well as sleeping cars. Over most of continental Europe the tinkling bell of the restaurant car conductor summoning passengers to lunch or dine was a familiar sound on a long-distance journey. These cars and his sleeping cars travelled in company with the rolling stock of the various European railways, but some trains were formed throughout of the Wagons-Lits company's vehicles and were known as *trains de luxe*. Both Nagelmackers and Pullman moved on from sleeping cars to saloons for daytime travel, with armchair seating and attractive décor. These constituted the image of the *train de luxe* in the public mind. The standard Wagons-Lits two-berth sleeping compartment, convertible for day use, was convenient rather than luxurious, but with a restaurant car at hand it was a pleasant temporary home on a long journey.

Pullman's style of sleeping car did not find favour in Europe but his day saloons ran in certain trains and he had a manufacturing facility in Italy in Turin. Pullman cars were shipped in sections from the United States to England and erected at Derby for use on the Midland Railway's Anglo-Scottish trains. But they proved less popular than had been hoped and the company's contract with the Midland ended in 1888. Manufacture of Pullman Cars in England was then transferred to Brighton and cars from these works ran for many

In the late nineteenth century long train journeys offered comfort, elegance and refinement. The attention to detail was evident both in the sleeping compartment and in the restaurant car. The Compagnie Internationale des Wagons-Lits listed among its clients some of the most important crowned heads of the age. Today, despite the development of air transport over long distances, the train still offers the very real advantage to the traveller of enjoying a good meal and a sound night's sleep. The cars of the WL continue to link the principal European cities, while similar services are to be found in central and eastern Europe. The silverware and embroidered tablecloth, however, are relics of a bygone age.

years on the London, Brighton and South Coast Railway. Here they provided the catering service on the fast trains. One London–Brighton service was all-Pullman. This was the Southern Belle, steam-hauled from 1908 until 1934, by which time it was an electric train and had been renamed Brighton Belle. Many stage celebrities who lived on the coast returned home on the Brighton Belle at night, and when the service was withdrawn in 1972 a Pullman steward in reminiscent mood described at as "more like a club than a train." Some visitors to England were puzzled by the train in its electric form and occasionally were nearly left behind because they prolonged their goodbyes on the platform in the expectation that it would not depart until a locomotive had been coupled on.

George Pullman died in 1897. A British branch of the company was formed in 1906 and operated as an independent concern until taken over by British Railways nearly 60 years later.

Channel crossings were the least popular feature of travel between Britain and the Continent. For those who could afford first-class travel, the London–Paris journey was made more comfortable in 1929 when the Golden Arrow all-Pullman express began running between London and Dover. At the Channel it connected with a specially built steamship, the *Canterbury*, and at the other side of the Channel passengers were ushered into the Flèche d'Or, another all-Pullman train in which the journey to Paris was completed. In the depression years of the 1930s, however, the service lost some of its glamour when on the British side of the Channel ordinary first- and second- class coaches were included in the train.

A more original development in cross-

Below: Further evocations of the Belle Epoque in posters of health resorts. After the First World War the railways came to be subjected to increasing competition from other forms of transport. Even steam engines became more streamlined as can be seen by comparing two generations of American locomotives (opposite).

Channel communications took place shortly before the Second World War. By that time the British Pullman Car Company and Wagons-Lits were linked, having the same chairman. An overnight service of sleeping cars was introduced between London and Paris, the cars crossing the Channel on a train ferry vessel. The service was revived after the Second World War under the name Night Ferry but its traffic was increasingly eroded by air travel and it was withdrawn. The cars were the only Wagons-Lits vehicles built to suit the British loading gauge which is more restricted than on the Continental systems.

The bitter disputes between France and Germany, the European upheavals following the Congress of Berlin of 1878 and the Russo-Turkish disturbances in the Balkan peninsula failed to prevent the departure, on 4 October 1883, of the most famous train in the world, the Orient Express, which would survive the many

storms of the new century. The original line designated for this renowned proto-type was changed according to political circumstances of the time: it was first routed through Munich, Salzburg, Vienna and Budapest, and restricted to the Ro-manian side of the Danube, then diverted via Belgrade–Sofia, and only in 1889 able to cross the continent uninterruptedly on its classic route from the Seine to the Bos-phorus, offering its earliest passengers marvellous glimpses of the Alps, extensive vistas of the course of the Danube, and all the exoticism and mystery of Constantinople.

The most celebrated of these trains was the Simplon Orient. It skirted lakes and as day dawned through the carriage windows young couples could gaze dreamily and romantically at the shores of Lakes Geneva, Maggiore and Garda, at Venice from the bridge over the lagoon, and fi-nally at the city of Trieste. And the earliest honeymooners had as backcloth the cren-ellated white turrets of the Miramare castle, where Charlotte and Maximilian von Hapsburg spent their brief season of perfect happiness prior to the Mexican

episode, and where the Archduke Ferdinand was to pass a single night on his fateful journey from Konopiste to Sarajevo.

On 16 October 1871, a train pulled out of Paris, still not wholly recovered from the Jacobin fury of the Communards, on its inaugural direct journey to Rome, through the Fréjus Tunnel, the first of the great tunnels through the Alps. A little later there appeared on the scene the Nord Express from Ostend to Berlin. Here it split into two sections, one bound for Danzig, Vilna and St Petersburg, the other for Warsaw and Moscow. This city was the departure point for the legendary Trans-Siberian Express (a model of this train was exhibited at the Paris Exposition of 1900), initially going no farther than Tomsk, in the heart of the taiga, the route eventually being extended to Vladivostock.

In a bookshop in the Westbahnhof, Vienna, it is possible to buy a handsomely bound copy of the official Austro-Hungarian railway timetable which came into force in the summer of 1914 during the last peaceful weeks of the empire's existence. This includes pictures in it of the Prague–Grado link (trains stopped at the lagoon bridge according to a now vanished agreement), the Budapest–Fiume line, extended to the tiny station of Abbazia-Mattuglie, the Berlin–Naples route (on the international pages) and the longer stretch from St Petersburg to Cannes.

These direct trains obviously catered for an élite: passengers who would take holidays in expensive resorts by the sea and in the mountains and leisurely journeys from one grand hotel to another during the high season.

Europe was never again to experience such happy conditions whereby a generation of travellers, even those of more

A revival of interest in the glamour of a bygone age led to the relaunching of a luxury version of the Orient Express, on the traditional routes from London to Paris and Venice. Recently one of these trains, accurately reconstructed down to the smallest detail, made an exceptional round trip from Paris to Tokyo via Berlin, Moscow, Peking and Hong Kong.

modest means, were able to cross from one end of the continent to another without passports, armed merely with a laissez-passer and transit permit. Only the arrival of commercial air transport would bring about a curtailment of standard travelling times, and only the expansion of roads and highways would result in the movement of even greater numbers of holiday-makers.

But from the viewpoint of the railways, despite cooperation between national networks in East and West which would prevail even in the most critical stages of the cold war, certain travel facilities were no longer practicable.

Although in the West the TEE and later the Eurocity lines were to contribute powerfully to international traffic – still accompanied by the splendid Wagons-Lits, imitated beyond the Iron Curtain by the Mitropa – the beneficial effects of high-speed travel are now mainly associated with internal routes.

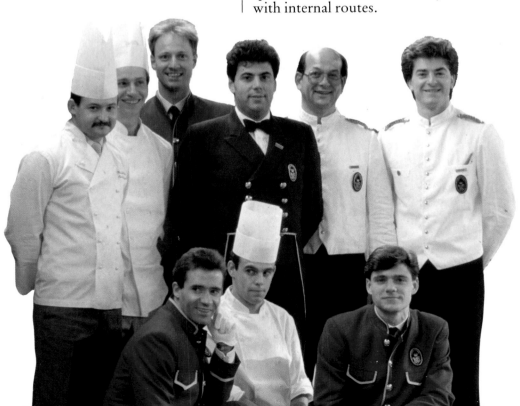

It is true that free flow of traffic and through tickets make it possible to travel comfortably from, say, Athens to Dublin, but nevertheless in order to go from Trieste to Ljubljana or from Regensburg to Pilsen passengers lose a couple of hours as a result of engine-changes and double customs inspections.

Travel was altogether a much simpler affair at the beginning of the twentieth century.

THE CLIMACTIC YEARS

At the dawn of the Roaring Twenties Europe was still recovering from the Great War. France once more had frontier stations on the Rhine, with Strasbourg and Saint Louis outside Basle. She also won back the Tavannes Tunnel which had been the vital pillar at the glory of Verdun. The central imperial powers emerged dismem-

Below: The 280 of the Ferrovie Nord, Milan, dating from the 1930s. In the early years of the twentieth century, the cities of the Great Lakes region in America had reached the peak of their industrial expansion, before being rudely awakened by the shock of the Depression.

Opposite: An advertising poster of the Cincinnati, Hamilton and Dayton Rail Road.

bered and from their ashes rose the national states of central Europe, with their respective railway systems. America was at this time entering upon a spectacularly dynamic period of history; this applied also to her legendary locomotives, which puffed and shrilled with explosive impatience in the steam-filled stations buried in the precious subsoil of Chicago and New York.

Railway expansion reached its zenith in 1928, the year when the world's networks (measured in thousands of kilometers) registered the following totals:

North America	*510*
South America	*92*
Europe	*385*
Asia	*140*
Africa	*68*
Oceania	*50*

for a total of 1,245,000 km of track, more or less the same as applies today, but only because the expansion of railways in Africa and Asia compensated for the collapse in North America following the crash of 1929 and the slight regression elsewhere.

As for Europe, the same period brings to light the following data:

Germany	*56.3*
France	*51*
States born from the dismembering of the central powers	*45*
Great Britain	*34*
Italy	*22*

It was above all in Europe, therefore, thanks to the advantages of electrification and the wide-scale diffusion of heat traction that the train enjoyed increasing success during the thirties.

As soon as the principle of electromagnetism was discovered, inventors tried to put it to practical use for driving machinery. The earliest recorded example of electric traction on rails dates from 1842 when Robert Davidson demonstrated a locomotive on the Edinburgh and Glasgow Railway in Scotland. At about this time he organized an exhibition of "Electro-magnetism as a Moving Power." A handbill advertising this event can be seen in the Science Museum in London, but apart from stating that it was under the patronage of the Royal Scottish Society of Arts it gives no details of where it was to take place or when. The locomotive illustrated on the handbill is a four-wheel trolley on which most of the space is taken up by a battery. Electromagnets powered by the battery attracted or repelled iron bars attached to a drum on the axle, causing it to revolve. This arrangement is known to have moved the locomotive at up to 4 mph (6.4 kmh) but the power would have been very

limited and it is doubtful whether the public enjoyed the promised spectacle of "A Locomotive Engine Carrying Passengers on a Circular Railway." Davidson's machine is said to have been destroyed by angry workers whose livelihood depended on the steam locomotive. If this occurred before the exhibition it may have saved him embarrassment.

Practical electrification did not begin until the invention of the dynamo and the electric motor. The first electric line with the rudiments of the electric railway as we know it was demonstrated by its inventor, Werner von Siemens, at the Berlin Industrial Exhibition in 1879. Drawings show that passengers were carried in open four-wheel carriages, each with a central bench on which passengers sat back to back.

Public transport with electric traction began in Great Britain when Magnus Volk opened his electric railway on the sea front at Brighton in 1883. This was really a tramway although the cars had their own track and did not run along the front itself. The first line in Great Britain on which the trains were hauled by electric locomotives was the underground City and South London Railway, opened in 1890. Electrification by the British main-line railways was confined for many years to suburban services round London, Manchester, Liverpool and Newcastle-on-Tyne. By the 1930s, however, the London suburban network of the Southern Railway had been extended so far that only 36 miles (58 km) more would bring it to the coast at Brighton. The decision to electrify over this distance was taken and from 1 January 1933 all London–Brighton main-line passenger trains were worked by electricity, although steam locomotives continued to haul freight and to operate passenger

service on secondary routes.

In the United States Thomas Edison was interested in railway electrification at an early stage. He opened an experimental line in the grounds of his Menlo Park laboratories in New Jersey in 1880, on which a small locomotive pulled two small cars at speeds up to 40 mph (64.4 kmh). After other inventors and engineers had laid a solid groundwork, an important step forward was taken in 1895 when the Baltimore and Ohio Railroad electrified a steeply graded section of main line in Baltimore and worked both passenger and freight traffic with electric locomotives. One reason for electrification was the presence on the route of a long and steeply graded tunnel in which smoke and steam would have caused problems. The Baltimore city authorities would not allow any ventilation holes or openings in any street or avenue.

There were similar problems in New York where smoke and cinders from steam locomotives greatly annoyed lineside residents in Manhattan, while in a tunnel approaching the Grand Central station smoke and steam often made it impossible to read signals, leading to a number of accidents. Electric traction on this section of line began in 1906. Electric locomotives hauled the trains as far as Harmon, 33 miles (53 km) from Grand Central, where steam locomotives took over. Electric locomotives were now seen at the head of all the express trains on the New York–Chicago main line.

The Pennsylvania Railroad began electrifying suburban services at Philadelphia in 1915. In 1930 the main line from Philadelphia to Trenton was converted and this section formed the first part of the eventual electrification from New York through to Washington, completed in 1935. The

Opposite: An English railway worker of the Southern Railways clad in a 1930s-style uniform stands beside the boiler of a steam locomotive. In almost all the European countries and in America the railway trade unions, since the end of the nineteenth century, have been traditionally among the most staunch of all unions in the protection of their members' rights.

Pennsylvania's main line from New York to Chicago left the Washington line at Trenton and was electrified as far as Harrisburg. Progress towards an all-electric New York–Chicago route was halted by the Second World War. It was not resumed because of the rapid advance of diesel power.

The two principal systems of electrification throughout the world have been with direct current or alternating current. An alternating current system may use a single-phase or a three-phase supply. The Pennsylvania electrification was at 15,000V alternating current, single-phase. The longest direct current electrification in the USA was on the Milwaukee Road from Harlowtown to Avery, 438 miles (705 km), crossing the Belt Mountains, the main range of the Rockies, and the Bitter Root Mountains.

The three-phase alternating current system has the advantages of using motors of simple and sturdy construction, similar to most industrial machines, together with the ability to return power automatically to the supply system if a train on a down gradient tries to accelerate above the speed selected by the driver. This has a braking effect and holds the speed of the train steady, while contributing power to a train ascending the gradient. The drawback, however, is that two overhead wires are necessary and the range of speed available to the driver is limited. The system has been used on steeply graded routes, mostly in Northern Italy. At one time the Great Northern Railway in the United States operated trains with three-phase alternating current on its steep gradients – as much as 1 in 25 – where the line crossed the Cascade Mountains.

Engineers have never entirely aban-

During the 1930s the railways were engaged in a variety of jobs that were later taken over by road vehicles. *Opposite:* A policeman in Berlin at the time of the Weimar Republic halts the traffic to let through a goods train being used in the construction of a new street. *Below:* The Dresden Opera House, completely destroyed in the aerial bombardment of February 1945, and subsequently rebuilt entirely on the lines of the original plan. Dresden was decimated by the bombing. Its main station, the terminus for trains carrying Silesian refugees fleeing the advance of Soviet troops, was destroyed.

doned the idea of using three-phase motors for traction. In the last few years this has become possible without the drawbacks of inflexible speed control and a complicated overhead system. Three-phase traction motors can now be installed in locomotives whatever the form of current supply since today this can be changed to three-phase by means of electronic inverters.

For many years electric railways generated their own power supplies and provided their own distribution systems. Countries with hydroelectric power, such as Switzerland, Germany and Austria, took advantage of this natural resource to electrify main lines earlier than countries which had to build coal-fired power stations. The development of national power systems later put an abundant source of power within the railways' reach but there were technical problems in the

way of using it. Experiments to overcome the problems were begun by the German State Railway on a line in the Black Forest in the late 1930s but they were interrupted by the Second World War. After the war the line came into the French zone of occupation and French engineers took up the work again. They finally perfected a practical system for enabling electric railways to use power at the industrial frequency of 50Hz (cycles per second). There was no longer a need for separate railway power systems and the economics of railway electrification were transformed.

The steam locomotive is remembered with affection but it was finally unable to compete efficiently with other forms of power. Its performance depended greatly on the skills of drivers and firemen, and in particular on the physical ability of the fireman to shovel large quantities of coal when high power outputs had to be sustained. After the invention of the diesel engine by Dr Rudolf Diesel, experiments were made using it for railway traction but the early diesel engines were heavy, slow-running machines and the locomotives were used mainly for shunting. An exception was a "universal" locomotive for main-line passenger and freight services built by the British firm of Armstrong Whitworth in the 1930s. It was tested on the London and North Eastern Railway but the management was not convinced of the reliability of diesel power and after an engine failure had confirmed their fears the locomotive was withdrawn.

A more dramatic development was the building of a two-car diesel train for the German State Railway in 1932. It was powered by two 12-cylinder diesel engines of 410 hp which were fast running and lighter than previous types. When the train began

service between Berlin and Hamburg in 1933 a new epoch in European inter-city travel began. The unit, called the Fliegende Hamburger, covered the 178.1 miles (270 km) at an average speed of 77.4 mph (124.6 kmh), which was the fastest regular schedule in the world at that time. Moreover, because of speed restrictions on some parts of the route, others had to be covered at 99.6 mph (160 kmh). This was the first time such a speed had to be maintained daily to keep to the timetable. Several other trains of similar design followed.

Some very fast runs were being made by steam at this period. In the United States there was keen competition between three railroads operating between Chicago and the twin cities of St Paul and Minneapolis. On 20 July 1934 the Chicago, Milwaukee, St Paul and Pacific Railroad (usually called the Milwaukee Road) threw down a challenge by showing that the 85 miles (136.8 km) between Chicago and Milwaukee could be covered in a fraction over $67^{1}/_{2}$ minutes. Within a month all three lines were cutting the journey time from Chicago to St Paul from about 10 hours to $6^{1}/_{2}$ hours. The Milwaukee Road and the Chicago and North Western relied on steam, the Milwaukee building a special locomotive and train, while the C&NW used a "hotted up" version of an existing locomotive. The Chicago, Burlington and Quincy entrusted the new schedules to diesel power, having already gained experience with its Pioneer Zephyr.

All this led to the building of more powerful locomotives capable of hauling a nine-coach train weighing 388 tonnes. The fastest run by this train was made when the eastbound train covered the 85 miles from Milwaukee to Chicago in $69^{1}/_{2}$ minutes, maintaining 100 mph (160 kmh) for 31 miles (49.9 km) and twice reaching 110 mph (177 kmh).

In Great Britain Gresley's Coronation schedule of 6 hours from London Kings Cross to Edinburgh brought a quick response from the London, Midland and Scottish Railway's West Coast Route from London Euston to Glasgow. The distance here was 401.4 miles (645.7 km) compared with 392.7 miles (631.6 km) from Kings Cross to Edinburgh and the going was harder, but with new streamlined locomotives and updated rolling stock the LMS introduced a schedule of 6½ hours for its Coronation Scot express. Before the Coronation Scot went into service a demonstration run was made from Euston to Crewe which is celebrated in British Railway history. The train topped a rise at 93.5 mph (150.4 kmh) and then raced down the gradient towards Crewe with rapidly rising speed. It had reached 114 mph (183.4 kmh) by the time it was necessary to slow for the station stop. It

Railways have been both the heroes and the victims of war.

Opposite and below: Pictures of the celebrated bridge over the River Kwai which the Japanese forced prisoners of war to build through the Siamese jungle so that their trains could get through directly to Burma. This railway of death, so called because of the terrible cost in human life involved in its construction, was to have an unhappy fate. Planned as a link between Bangkok and Rangoon, it was destroyed at various points during the war and was never repaired. Today Thai trains run only as far as Nam Tok, just beyond the fateful bridge.

almost seemed that the driver had left it too late and the train swayed alarmingly as it negotiated the crossovers approaching the platform, with sparks streaming from screeching brake blocks. Happily the only casualties were some plates and saucers in the restaurant car.

A few days after the Coronation Scot's exploit, guests were invited to sample the Coronation on a trial run. They included many members of the press who were hoping for a stirring reply to the LMS record, but they were disappointed when railway officials went through the train before departure to announce that there would be no attempt to exceed the normal service

speeds. The run was therefore a relatively sedate affair.

Gresley's riposte came later, and in much less public circumstances. On 3 July 1938 the streamlined locomotive Mallard was engaged on braking trials with passenger coaches. As before, full throttle was used to climb to the top of a "hump," which was surmounted at 74.5 mph (119.9 kmh). Once over the top speed soared on the falling gradient, eventually touching the world record for steam of 126 mph (202.7 kmh). It is now known that the record attempt was premeditated but kept secret until it was successful.

Had it not been for the Second World War the Mallard record might have been challenged. The fact that the speed was attained on a 1 in 200 down gradient has not dimmed its fame but it has left the door open for debate. Two years earlier a German locomotive hauling a special train of five vehicles, with invited passengers on board, touched 118 mph (190 kmh) on level track between Berlin and Hamburg.

In the last years of steam in the United States some unconventional and interesting high-speed designs were seen but the diesel was gaining the ascendant from the time the Electromotive Division of General Motors developed a compact, fast-revving engine in which the high crankshaft speed gave a power/weight ratio which eclipsed its contemporaries. Powered by this engine, the Burlington's Pioneer Zephyr on 26 May 1934 made a startling non-stop demonstration run of 1,015.4 miles (3,243.5 km), ending in Chicago at the Century of Progress Exposition, where the train was put on display beside the Union Pacific's M-10000 diesel train. This was the prelude to the Burlington's Denver Zephyr and Union Pacific's City of Los Angeles

Strikes of employees, although often motivated by the wish to defend and improve services, sometimes result in the railways losing customers. *Below:* Railway staff chatting on the platform during a stoppage at Clapham Junction, London, on 29 May 1955. This is still one of the world's busiest stations, handling some 2,000 trains every day.

with other Zephyr and City services to follow.

In the early diesel expresses the power car was an integral part of a streamlined set of vehicles. By 1938 separate diesel locomotives were coming into service. Such a locomotive could consist of a "cab" unit with a driving position and "booster" units, controlled from the cab, according to the total power required. Locomotives were now rolling off the Electromotive production lines and in a few years' time were being sold "off the shelf" to railways all over the world.

THE RAILWAYS IN WARTIME

The silence of a warm summer's night in 1937 was shattered by the explosion of a Japanese bomb placed between the sleepers of the railway near Shenyang in Manchuria, in what could be interpreted as a prologue to the more massive world war then looming. Two years later the winds of war swept towards Europe.

The episode received little publicity in the context of other hostile events which proved to be precursors of the tragic escalation of ferocity which was to flout all rules of law and international agreements. The campaign in Poland was over in less

Below: The entrance to Milan's Stazione Nord in the 1930s, showing day trippers about to embark on the short journey north to the lakes.

than a month, demonstrating the crucial role assumed by the air force. The bombing of Warsaw on 17 September 1939 spared the civilian quarters and cut lines of communication with military precision, so that the railway system of the Polish capital was almost completely disrupted on both banks of the Vistula, and it was at least 20 years before the three main stations – Centralna, Wilenska and Gdanska – returned to their former state of efficiency.

But on 10 May 1940 an inexplicable air attack was made on the station at Freiburg in southern Germany, when 11 bombs caused the deaths of several people awaiting the train from Basle. The bombing of

this lovely Rhenish town, particularly dear to Hitler, was attributed to the Germans themselves, for people still recalled the Machiavellian attempt to legitimize the attack on Poland by means of a frontier incident provoked by the SS, which had destroyed the radio station at Gleiwitz, in the free territory of Danzig. So it was rumoured that the Freiburg operation might have been staged as an alibi for the massive and indiscriminate aerial attack four days later on Rotterdam.

By now it was total war. France was overrun in the following month: in the hour of final defeat, on the evening of 13 June, the last trains left Austerlitz station in Paris, bound for the very same destinations that panic-stricken bourgeois refugees had made for back in 1870 and 1914: Tours, Bordeaux and Perpignan. The German advance guards found the cafés on the Champs Elysées doing lively business but the stations deserted, and at 19.10 the clock of the Gare St Lazare, last departure point for Le Havre and England, stopped. But a patrol kept watch right up to the time of its recapture – whether by the regular army, Vichy collaborators or Resistance fighters – on the Fades viaduct over the Sioule gorge, the highest in Europe, with a 436-ft (133-m) span, built by the famous engineer Alexandre Gustave Eiffel.

The railways were now primary objectives and chosen targets: the fury of German might was soon directed against Great Britain, with the aerial onslaught of autumn 1940: London was bombed for 86 consecutive nights, except for Sunday 3 November, when impenetrable cloud halted the attack. The capital was pounded without remission and all 16 stations, without exception, were devastated. Four years later the indiscriminate individual attacks

of the flying bombs only hit Fenchurch Street, Euston and Charing Cross stations, and the Metropolitan Railway tunnels were to be transformed into armaments factories.

The conflict flared up in many different countries. After the attack on Pearl Harbor, Japan's armed forces struck out in all directions, from the borders of India to the shores of distant Australia, supporting the ground advance with the construction by forced labour of the "death railway" from Bangkok to Rangoon, commemorated in the epic pages of Pierre Boulle's *The Bridge on the River Kwai*. Meanwhile in Europe, after the furious battle amid the rubble of the October Revolution locomotive works at Stalingrad, the hour of reckoning arrived for the Axis powers.

In their assault on the Third Reich the Allies also chose trains and rail networks as prime objectives. On the night of 30 May 1943, for example, there was an air attack on Wuppertal, in which the famous mono-rail suspension railway was hit; and on 23 October there was a raid on the Henschel locomotive works – which carried on their tenders the empty boast of "everything for the Führer and victory" – doing considerable damage to the city of Kassel.

Opposite: The extraordinary and unstoppable development of private motoring is at the root of the perennial crisis that has affected the railways since the end of the Second World War. It would lead inevitably to major traffic jams, as this photograph of the entrance to a major river bridge in America during the 1950s illustrates. The equally rapid advance of civil aviation also contributed to the steady decline of the train.

When a train loaded with explosives was hit from the air in Darmstadt station, part of the city's residential section was destroyed, as were all the bridges of Mainz: both were diversionary raids in preparation for one of the fiercest air raids on Frankfurt. Nearby Wiesbaden, however, where the nation's only factory turning out crematoria was located, remained untouched.

The railway corridor of Hamburg was destroyed by a storm of incendiary bombs on the night of 25 July 1943 (at the precise moment when Mussolini, Hitler's staunch ally, was overthrown in Rome), despite the decoy of a fake bridge behind the Lombardsbrücke facing the Dammtor station. In the post-war desolation, before the astonishing revival of the Hanseatic city, stark signs of the disaster remained for some time, as the shattered façade of the Hauptbahnhof looked out over a vast area of rubble dominated by the surviving bell tower of St Nicholas, reflected in the Alster like a sinister Lutheran profile. The heart of Munich's rail system also remained out of action for a long time – from the complex central network to the outlying stations of Pasing and Laimer – as a result of the prolonged heavy attack on the night of 25 April 1944.

41

Dresden was subjected to violent bombardment – 135,000 people were killed when 3,000 tons of bombs were dropped in two consecutive days – and seemed to be reduced to a skeleton on 14 February 1945, the corpses including those of children, who had sought shelter in the Hauptbahnhof, previously unscathed, but now the terminus for various trains carrying refugees from Silesia fleeing the advance of Soviet troops. The survivors had taken shelter behind the station but had been overcome by the fireball and hurricane generated by the intense heat.

At 17.10 on 21 April 1945 the last train left the Anhalter Bahnhof, one of Berlin's imposing main-line stations, and managed to reach Soviet-occupied Prague prior to the city's being surrounded, by way of Dresden's Friedrichstadtbahnhof, which had survived the February raid. A piece of the terminal's façade still remains as testimony to the horrors of war, surrounded by vast empty spaces, bridges and loop-lines, until recently in the sinister shadow of the Wall.

It was now spring and the heat speeded up the decomposition of unburied bodies, while the birds twittered in the Tiergarten and the Berlin Philharmonic punctually began its Sunday afternoon concert. In the battered hall on the Potsdamerplatz the pistons of that last locomotive shrieked out a counterpoint to the bark of machine-guns.

The railways were badly hit by the Second World War. Events had demonstrated how vulnerable they were, whereas road transport was already benefiting from the reconversion of wartime industry to civil use. Reconstruction of the rail networks, though soon underway, was to be a

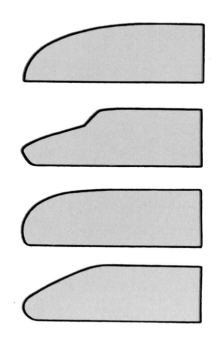

From the 1970s, initially in Japan and then in France, Italy and Germany, the train set up records for speed, while the automobile was increasingly restricted in this area; an imposition of speed limits sought to contain the daily accident toll on the roads, all too often caused by speeding.

Opposite: One of the ICE trains destined for commercial service in the Federal German Republic. In spring 1988, during a trial on the new Hanover–Würzburg line, this train broke the speed record previously held by the TGV, for the first time exceeding 250 mph (400 kmh) and proving that the technical resources of the traditional railway are far from exhausted.

long and difficult process, sometimes left unfinished.

THE GREAT CRISIS

"Commodore Vanderbilt ... gone, Jeffersonian ... gone, The Twentieth Century Limited ... gone." A glance through American books on the history of the railroads is to become immersed in the gloomy atmosphere of *Spoon River Anthology*. One after another, in the space of a few years, the glorious and prestigious express trains disappeared, following the sad fate that had already overtaken the peripheral Interurban networks which in their golden years travelled from New York to Boston without any solution as to their continuity. Photographs document the last journeys, with the coloured cook moved to tears and the placard attached to the last carriage bearing the word "Goodbye" or "Adios."

After the Second World War the collapse of the North American railroad system – which had been under heavy pressure from the volume of goods and numbers of passengers carried – gathered pace as a result of the astonishing expansion of civil aviation and the powerful mass attraction of motoring, already established among the middle class 20 years beforehand with the introduction by Henry Ford of his Model T. In Europe, where the wartime railways had gone through a long and difficult recovery period, the train managed to resist the competition better, thanks mainly to government subsidies, but here too the decline appeared to be irreversible.

Above all, the development of the highway systems led to a railway crisis. The new ribbons of asphalt, planned and constructed by means of techniques that were

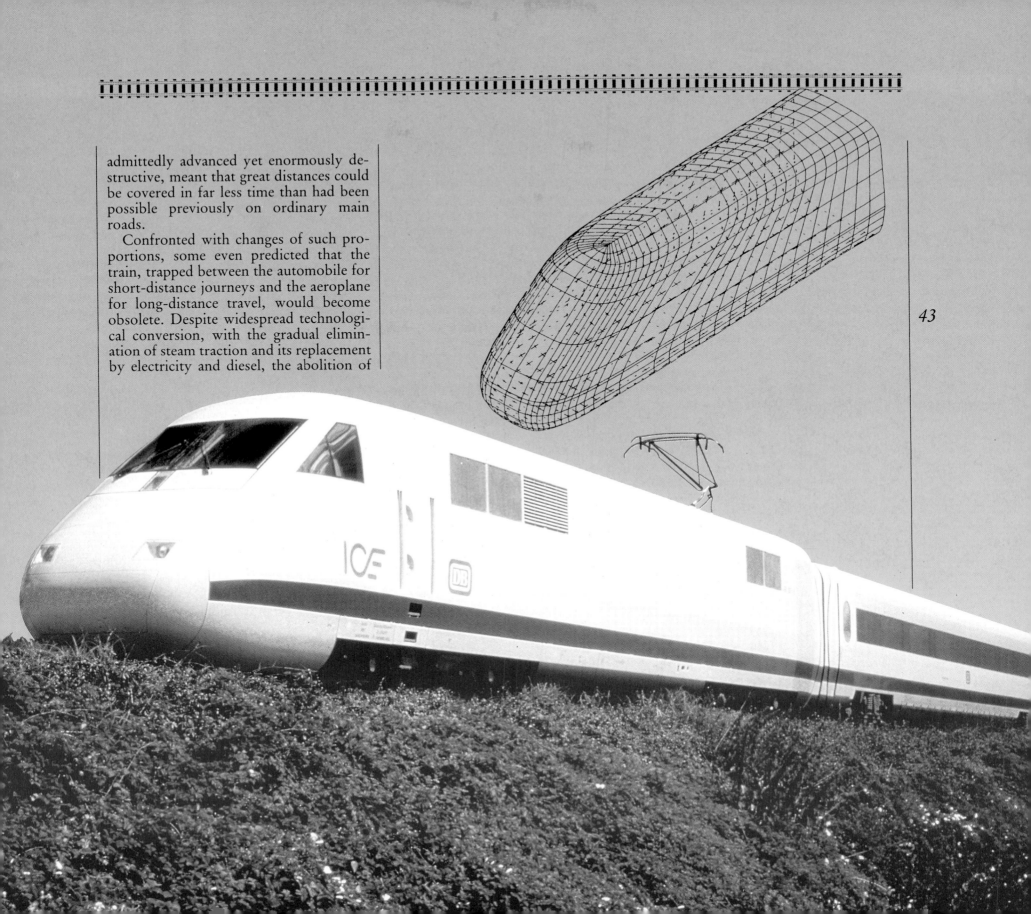

admittedly advanced yet enormously de-
structive, meant that great distances could
be covered in far less time than had been
possible previously on ordinary main
roads.

Confronted with changes of such proportions, some even predicted that the
train, trapped between the automobile for
short-distance journeys and the aeroplane
for long-distance travel, would become
obsolete. Despite widespread technological conversion, with the gradual elimin-
ation of steam traction and its replacement
by electricity and diesel, the abolition of

43

third-class services and the launch of the Trans-Europe Express, by the end of the 1950s the railways had not managed to keep pace with their rivals. This meant fewer passengers and goods, less revenue and greater deficits.

The hasty and superficial solutions frequently proposed for saving what could be saved sometimes led to drastic reductions of personnel (in Germany between 1954 and 1980 the staff level fell from 482,000 to 326,000) and the wholesale closure of lines, as in Great Britain, where the mileage in service was halved.

There was then serious talk about the "death of the railway," with discussions as to ways of reconverting intercity lines to metropolitan or monorail systems, at that time the only ones that seemed to have a guaranteed future.

A PHOENIX RISES AGAIN

Following the Yom Kippur war in 1973 and the consequent oil embargo imposed by the Arab countries, some European governments were forced to introduce various austerity measures, among them the prohibition of Sunday motoring, an action which did not lead to the expected avalanche of protest but was welcomed almost as a form of liberation.

Thought was therefore given to ways of reviving rail transport. France was the first nation to take up the challenge of Japan, where the Shinkansen trains had since 1964 linked Tokyo and Osaka (332 miles/553 km) in under three hours. The fast Paris–Lyons line, begun in 1976, was completed in 1983, enabling the TGV (Trains à Grande Vitesse) to reduce the time for the journey between the two cities by a couple

Great Britain, even though it has not yet built high-speed lines (the first is planned for the stretch between London and the future Channel Tunnel), possesses trains capable of reaching 125 mph (200 kmh) in regular service.

Opposite: A retired engine driver stands beside an HST (High Speed Train) under the Victorian roof of Paddington station, London, 30 April 1975.

Below: One of the first prototypes of a train with inclinable body, capable of negotiating small-radius curves at high speeds.

of hours; previously the excellent TEE took four hours to travel the distance of more than 300 miles (500 km). The new trains won back half the clients who had previously chosen to travel the same route by air.

Major new railway enterprises were launched between the late seventies and early eighties: the Belgrade–Bar in Yugoslavia, the Swiss Furka Tunnel, and the Baikal–Amur in eastern Siberia. Others were in progress or at planning stage, with a strong likelihood of seeing the light by the end of the century, including the last TGV lines to the Atlantic and Germany. The most ambitious project of all, of which some had dreamed for two centuries, was the tunnel under the English Channel.

Yet the gigantic Anglo-French undertaking no longer constituted a record. The tireless Japanese had excavated a tunnel 34 miles (57 km) long under the Seikan Strait, and today trains run between Tokyo and Sapporo without the inconvenience of ferry crossings. And the four large islands that make up the Japanese archipelago are now no longer separated, thanks to the continuous rail links through underwater tunnels that link Honshu with Kyushu to the south and Hokkaido to the north, as well as, most recently, the bridge to Shikoku.

So at long last the railways can shed their nostalgic image and take their rightful place of honour again in the annals of world transport. Nostalgia for the steam railway, however, dies hard. In Great Britain there are some 70 preservation sites where steam locomotives can be seen in action or on display, thanks to the dedication of volunteers who carry out every kind of task from repair and maintenance of locomotives and permanent way to selling tickets.

CHAPTER 2

TRAINS IN ART AND LITERATURE

46 There is an enormous body of literature devoted to the subject of railways. In many countries, for example, there are bookshops that specialize in this field, and even general bookstores have special sections for trains.

Most of these works, often documented in great detail, concentrate on the technical and historical story of railway development, on individual lines or on rolling stock. In those countries which boast the biggest number of specialists and enthusiasts, there is keen interest even in associated aspects of the subject, such as signalling. There are clubs which hold expert discussions on the "decauville" lines and the London Metropolitan.

Although less widespread, there has always been interest, too, in exploring the relationship between railways and the arts. Technical considerations have perhaps tended to obscure the aesthetic aspects of the world of rail. Yet art, in its many forms, is uniquely equipped to mea-sure the true impact of the "Iron Horse" on contemporary civilization.

This chapter, therefore, is devoted to a brief survey of the role assumed by railways in literature, architecture, music, painting, photography and film. As it is a personal selection, it will inevitably be controversial and incomplete.

We have omitted sculpture because books specializing in this art form are better able to convey the subject's monumentality and self-glorification. In fact, the finest concrete monument is often the train itself, whether in motion, at a station platform or even in a museum. This last option may well be the only one for many of the finest steam locomotives which have disappeared in recent years. Seen thus, anchored to a brief section of track, they may look rather sad but nevertheless they serve to remind us, amid the bustle of modern life, of the glories of a vanished age.

THE "MONSTER" IN LITERATURE

If you are someone who does not enjoy looking at the countryside or chatting to fellow passengers you will no doubt bury yourself in a book while the train speeds along. The habitual train traveller is far more fortunate than the person who goes everywhere by car or by air; the former is prisoner to the map or guide, and the latter, unless on a long intercontinental flight, can only thumb through the main features of a newspaper. The thriller is one of those literary genres ideally suited to the train, which might have been devised specifically to cater for the tastes and habits of the rail passenger.

The relationship between railway and literature is a long and happy one, for the subject is one amply documented in the works of many writers. Since it would be impossible to cover the entire range, a few brief notes and observations must suffice.

The autobiography of Mark Twain, published posthumously in 1924, mentions two important influences in the American novelist's life: one was the appearance of Halley's comet, the other the part played by trains in shaping a couple of decisive events. On the first occasion Twain recalls his job in one of the earliest railway yards in the West; the second, long afterwards, is a series of conferences which send him on a journey, in the early years of the present century, from one railway station to another, in a foretaste of the "on the road" culture of half a century later. In one of his stories Twain has the passengers of the Chicago–St Louis express trapped overnight in pitch darkness as a snowstorm rages outside.

Twain died at almost the same time as the legendary Tolstoy, whose magnificent

descriptions of the boundless steppes, the cares and aspirations of the Russian peasantry and the sense of freedom that imbues old age, are set against a background of trains whistling and roaring across the plains. This theme was both prophetic (in *Sebastopol*, for example, he pointed out that trains were already being used for military purposes) and obsessive, as in *Anna Karenina*, *The Kreutzer Sonata* and *Resurrection*. The great novelist was to die at a nondescript little railway station in Russia.

Other nineteenth-century writers also took up the theme. Henry James, special correspondent for *Atlantic Monthly*, voiced his disappointment at the Florence–Rome line which stopped at the Etruscan towns of Chiusi and Orvieto but not at the much nobler cities of Perugia and Assisi, relegated to a minor branch line. Many American authors hailed the arrival of the locomotive, including Emerson, Hawthorne, Thoreau and Whitman. American literature was to associate the train with the desire to roam freely in search of the new frontier of the West, culminating in the work of Jack Kerouac.

Heinrich Heine, Rhenish by birth and French by adoption, was seduced by the horizons that appeared beyond his adored Montmartre, thanks to the opening of the lines of Rouen and Orléans, along which he dreamed in vain of travelling with his beloved Elisa von Krientz, in the *Französische Zustände*. The refined Proust, too, in his *À la Recherche du Temps Perdu*, was to transform the train into a charming imaginative microcosm. Kindred spirits in this achievement were Cendrars in his *Notes de Route*, the poets Neruda, Valery Larbaud and Yevtushenko, all of whom celebrated the train in their work.

Many works in English literature have

On the previous page: A frame from *Rotaie*, an Italian silent film made in 1928.

Opposite page: Typical view of a nineteenth-century station platform.

Below: A young woman gazes dreamily out of the window of the restaurant car at the passing landscape.

used the railway as a setting for certain incidents or have woven it into the plot. In Elizabeth Gaskell's *Cranford* one of the characters is killed by a train while saving a child. In Mrs Henry Wood's *East Lynne*, published in 1861, a railway accident is essential to an improbable plot in which the heroine's injuries give her the excuse to wear dark glasses and return unrecognized as governess to her son. Charles Dickens, born in 1812, lived well into the railway age, dying in 1870. In *Pickwick Papers* Mr Weller senior relates an alarming experience on his first railway journey when he found himself locked in a carriage with a "living widder" but on this occasion both survived the ordeal with unblemished reputations. In other works by Dickens the railway is seen in a more somber light. In *Dombey and Son* the villain, Carker, is struck down by a train as he flees from

justice. The short story *The Signalman* tells of a haunted tunnel and a railway accident. Dickens had first-hand experience of a serious derailment when travelling in a boat train from Dover in 1865. The train left the track at Staplehurst, in Kent. Ten passengers were killed and 50 injured. Dickens, who was unharmed, helped in the rescue work and was presented with a piece of plate by the South Eastern Railway in recognition of his services. Part of the manuscript of *Our Mutual Friend* which he carried with him escaped damage. The incident is referred to in a famous postscript to the book.

George Borrow, nine years older than Dickens, had little sympathy with the conventional picture of the stagecoach driver as a stout and genial philosopher. He considered the men rapacious and, to passengers who could not afford a large tip, insulting. In *Romany Rye* he wrote: "It was time that these fellows should be disenchanted, and the time – thank Heaven – was not far distant." His vitriolic attack continued: "Let the craven dastards who used to curry favour with them and applaud their brutality, lament their loss now that they and their vehicles have disappeared from the roads . . ."

A nineteenth-century rail journey through the countryside on a sunny afternoon, puffs of white smoke from the engine drifting across the fields, may seem idyllic. The reality, however, could be quite different – a stuffy carriage, growing tedium, and fidgeting children complaining of heat and boredom. "Saki" (H. H. Munro) chose just such a setting for a short story. Two querulous children are travelling with their aunt, who tries to distract them by telling stories, but these are of an improving and educative nature and conse-

Details of objects, buildings and symbols associated with the railways.

Above: A bookplate depicting the cross-section of a rail.

Opposite: The entrance to a small local station in northern Italy and a former baggage cart, now decorated with bowls of flowers. These somewhat romantic images, all but vanished in the stations of big cities, now only survive in small country stations which have not yet succumbed to automation.

quently clearly despised. When a young man in the carriage offers to try his hand at a story the proposal is accepted with relief. But not for long. His story is of a very good little girl who has been rewarded for her goodness by the prince of her country with a string of medals setting forth her virtues, and she is privileged to walk in his private park. While engaged in this exercise one day, proudly displaying her medals, a hungry wolf in search of its dinner comes on the scene. The child prudently hides behind a bush, but she is of a nervous disposition and her trembling causes her medals to clink together. The wolf is guided by the sound to her hiding place, with the inevitable consequences. This denouement is rapturously received by the children, whose sympathies are entirely with the wolf. Their aunt is less pleased. "I think it is a most improper story," she exclaims. The young man is saved from her wrath by the train arriving at his station. He alights, smiling inwardly at the embarrassment in store for the aunt when badgered in public by demands for "an improper story."

The railway has its place in poetry. "Is no foot of English ground secure from rash assault?" thundered Wordsworth when railway engineers invaded the Lake District. Tennyson was more forward looking. "Let the great world spin for ever down the ringing grooves of change" he wrote in *Locksley Hall*, his poetic vision of the future. By "ringing grooves" he is thought to have meant a railway, thinking that trains were guided by a grooved track.

Railways have also featured in some very bad verse. It is hard to think of a better example of bathos than a stanza from *The Bridgekeeper's Story*, a poem published in an old book of recitations by an author who preferred to remain anonymous. The bridgekeeper's duty was to close a swing bridge when a train was due. His little daughter would accompany him to watch it pass and wave to the passengers. One fatal day the child fell into the river at the very moment the train came into view. A quandary now confronted the bridge-keeper. Should he rescue his daughter or fulfil his duty to the railway company? He did both, as told in the following lines:

> Quick as thought then he flew to the
>   windlass
> And fastened the bridge with a crash
> And just as the train dashed across it
> He jumped in the screen with a splash

Drama and tension collapse with that last word.

It is noted elsewhere that the cinema has made Emile Zola's railway novel, *La Bête Humaine*, widely known, although the film versions have been modified and updated from 1870 to the mid-1930s. The book itself is a curious mixture of crime, passion, mental instability and meticulous description of railway working. Zola rode on the footplate to watch engine crews at work, and his other railway detail is equally closely studied. The end of the book is pure melodrama. The Franco-Prussian war has broken out and a crowded troop train is taking soldiers to the front. The driver and fireman are rivals in love. The fireman picks a quarrel with his mate and a fight ensues, in the course of which both men fall on to the track and are killed by the train, their injuries being described in gruesome detail. Now driverless, the train rushes on. Frantic warnings are tele-graphed ahead when all signals to stop are ignored. The soldiers on board – Zola uses

the term "cannon fodder" – are either dozing or drunk, unaware of their peril. The book ends with the train hurling itself towards inevitable disaster.

Trains continue to feature freely in thrillers, including those written by such famous authors as Agatha Christie, Ian Fleming, Graham Greene and Georges Simenon, whose *Man Who Watched the Trains Go By* is a classic.

RAILWAY ARCHITECTURE

Although one may not agree with Cendrars' description of stations as "the most beautiful churches in the world," it is certain that at the end of the nineteenth century, when Positivism was all the rage, and with an unshakeable faith in the march of progress, railway architecture assumed almost holy dimensions. There is eloquent testimony to this in the Gothic spires of London's St Pancras station or of Bristol's Temple Meads, as also in the Nordbahnhof, Vienna. Elsewhere stations took on Arabic forms, as in Toledo in Spain, or were modelled on neoclassical lines. There were also so-called "mortuary stations," such as the one at Rookwood in Wales that was dismantled and rebuilt in Canberra, Australia, with angels from the Last Judgement there to welcome passengers on their last journey.

Railway building made a great impact on nineteenth-century town planning and stations virtually assumed the function of new city gates and secular temples to traffic. The station was a veritable temple in which the cults of speed and punctuality were worshipped. Today railway timetables continue to condition our movements to a certain degree, but a century

Opposite: The front of the Bullona station of the Ferrovie Nord, Milan. Located in a fairly central district of Milan, near the Trade Fair building, this small station still handles heavy commuter traffic but retains the architectural features of a bygone age. Note the fresco with the winged wheel, a recurrent theme of many railway buildings.
Below: The Berlin station of Nikolassee has the appearance of a Lutheran church.

or more ago they were revolutionary, unifying nations through the measurement of time. The slow rhythms of the sun were now relayed precisely by the hands of station clocks, often set on top of imposing structures, like new bell-towers of the

industrial age. Examples of these clock-towers can still be seen in the Gare des Bénédictins at Limoges, at Saint-Pierre in Ghent, and, of course, at the Gare de Lyon in Paris, the first landmark of the *"ville lumière"* for innumerable visitors from abroad.

Every station, naturally, reflects the social and economic context in which it was conceived, from the Hauptbahnhof in Zurich, which exudes financial solidity as unmistakably as the banks that surround it, to the Nordic harshness of the station at Helsinki, Finland, designed by Eliel Saarinen after a full-blooded national debate among the supporters of various styles. And although it goes without saying that many are ordinary buildings without any claim to originality, it is nonetheless true that certain railway lines offer a miniature compendium of architecture to the attentive traveller.

Ironically, it is in the Third World, rather than in Europe – where appallingly ugly modern structures have been erected on the sites formerly occupied by older, more distinguished buildings – that respect and feeling for the past, and the desire to preserve the original architectural styles, are most evident. Some of the smaller stations in Thailand are quite astonishing – one could even mistake them for Buddhist temples – while in Kuala Lumpur in Malaysia the impressive railway station, reminiscent of a British royal palace, is by far the most important building in the city. And there are innumerable and totally unexpected instances of this elsewhere.

The principal railway stations in the West have undergone many changes of fortune, not all of them for the good. Some, which have remained substantially

unaltered, furnish a strange contrast to the streamlined and colourful rolling stock to be found inside. Others have taken on modern features after radical reconstruction which has deprived them, among other things, of their enormous iron roofs. Examples of this include Montparnasse in Paris and Vienna's Franz Josef Bahnhof. Then there are those forming part of huge commercial complexes, such as Lyon Perrache and Utrecht. And finally, a few, closed to traffic, which have escaped the clutches of the developers by intelligent and imaginative conversion. The principal example of this is the Gare d'Orsay in Paris which has been felicitously transformed from a station into an enormous museum of nineteenth-century art.

A detailed examination of the infinite variations of architectural style to be found in the world of rail would fill whole volumes and still remain incomplete, leaving out many buildings that complement a train journey – the marvellous station hotels and the offices situated on squares and avenues that are an integral part of the urban scene. Nor have we space to dwell on the actual station interiors – like certain extraordinary waiting-rooms such as that of the Kazanski in Moscow – or on their decoration, so often redolent of local craft and culture, as in the case of the splendid *azulejos* that adorn stations in Portugal. The works of art are not necessarily confined to the buildings themselves, for they apply equally to tunnels (in England the approaches to certain tunnels look like veritable castles), bridges of all styles – which alone would merit an entire book – and the very lines built across mountain ranges and other natural barriers.

But here we should pause for thought. The railway burst on the scene like a whirl-

Opposite: A fanfare of the Bersaglieri greets the revived Orient Express in Milan Central Station on 15 October 1983. This station retains its iron roofing, a feature still very common elsewhere in Europe, notably in Great Britain.
Right: York railway station, England, in a photograph taken in 1877.
Below: The impressive iron vaults of Frankfurt's Hauptbahnhof, one of the main railway junctions of central Europe.

wind, profoundly altering both the lives and surroundings of people everywhere. Those metal tracks which cut through fields and valleys, running alongside the seashore, spanning rivers and piercing mountains, inevitably produced a very different landscape. It is hard for us to imagine the impact this must have made. This

unquestionably violent intrusion today seems almost imperceptible and of little account, thanks to the skills of those engineers who succeeded in integrating the railway lines harmoniously with the environment. Anyone who has seen the train descending the Gotthard or climbing the Semmering in Austria, who has admired the series of railway bridges and tunnels winding and spiralling through the Grisons cannot deny that a perfect symbiosis between nature and the works of man can be achieved. The façade of the Musée d'Orsay is still a landmark in Paris when seen from the opposite bank of the Seine. The grandiose style recalls the days when this was the terminus for long-distance expresses from Narbonne, Toulouse, Bordeaux and the Spanish border which were hauled by electric locomotives over the low-level line between Orsay and the Gare d'Austerlitz. There is still an Orsay station with its platforms below street level but the entrance is by an inconspicuous subway and the trains are cross-city services between suburban areas east and west of Paris. As part of this development the Orsay station has been linked with the nearby Gare des Invalides, fulfilling a long-standing plan for a rail connection between the two termini.

Below: A cross-section of the Gare d'Orsay after its refurbishment by Gae Aulenti.
Opposite: The interior of the same building, showing the central passage with an exhibition of sculpture. The former Parisian station is the most striking example of the re-use of a railway area; famous architects from all over the world helped to transform it into an art museum.

Some stations have acquired grandeur after modest beginnings. When opened in 1853, Antwerp Central was out of keeping with the stately buildings surrounding it. King Leopold II wanted to see a station combining the older architectural styles in the concourse with contemporary skills in the construction of the glass roof over the platforms. The work was given to the architect Louis de la Censerie, who studied the other great stations of the day in Berlin, Frankfurt and Strasbourg. His station was opened to traffic in 1899 but the work was not finished until about 1905. A preservation order was made in 1975. Meanwhile time and weather had taken their toll, particularly in the steelwork of the roof. There was talk of building a new station but it was later decided that it could be made safe by careful restoration and this work began in 1988.

In West Germany, the Stuttgart Hauptbahnhof (Hbf) has been designated a national monument. This was the last of the big terminal stations built by the German State Railway (Deutsche Reichsbahn) in the 1921–23 period. It is an impressive structure with a tower 190 ft (58 m) high and a central hall 656 ft (200 m) long, with two entrances. Today 14 shops in the

57

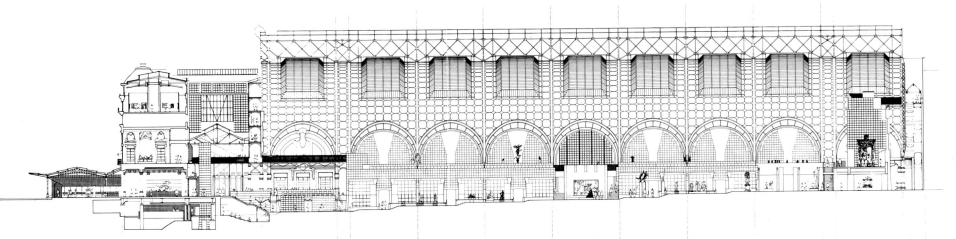

concourse selling everything from post-cards to more expensive articles are a source of useful rental revenue to the German Federal Railway (Deutsche Bundesbahn).

Another imposing façade is presented by Frankfurt Hauptbahnhof, which celebrated its centenary in 1988. There had been three terminal stations in the city but after the Franco-Prussian War it was decided to concentrate all traffic in one. A competition to find a suitable design attracted 55 entrants, from whom Herman Eggert of Strasbourg was declared the winner. When the station was opened in 1888 it was the largest in Europe. Crowds came to admire it, particularly the entrance hall, 75 ft (22.9 m) high and surmounted by a figure of Atlas supporting the globe, flanked by symbolic figures representing steam and electricity as the driving forces of world transport.

Below: Darius Milhaud, the French musician who wrote the score for the ballet, *Le train bleu*, in honour of that famous train.
Opposite: A train of the Ferrovie Nord, Milan, made up of old rolling stock. Some of these coaches are still in service on this local line in northern Italy, but they are gradually being replaced by new ones, some of them double-decker carriages.

THE RHYTHM OF THE TRAIN

Towards the close of the Romantic period, the train, roaring like an angry demon, threatened to shatter the peace of the countryside and disturb the calm of towns and cities. It was thus hardly an obvious source of musical inspiration for the composers of the time. Hegel had just advanced the theory in his *Aesthetics* at the University of Heidelberg that whereas the figurative arts manifested themselves in space, music was subjective, within the individual. Thus at first there were few compositions based on the rhythm or associated images of trains; but some did indeed leave their mark.

The earliest significant reference to railways in music was made by Gioacchino Rossini. One of his piano pieces, entitled *Un petit train de plaisir* – later included among the 14 *Péchés de vieillesse* – is a paraphrase of a train journey, rising to a crescendo to evoke the train's acceleration and with a deep, polytonal thud to simulate a derailment. Later, recognizable motifs associated with the souls of the likely victims of the disaster, reappear in the composer's *Stabat Mater* and *Petite Messe Solennelle*.

Another famous nineteenth-century figure, Johann Strauss Jr, who shared the position of court composer to his Imperial Majesty in Vienna with the mystical Anton Bruckner, paid two musical tributes to the train. The first was a polka called *Via Libera* and the second, one of his entrancing waltzes, *Eisenbahn Lust*, written to mark the opening of the steep Semmering line linking Vienna and Trieste.

Although one eminent critic has recently compared the noise of the train leaving a city to the initial lamentation of Bach's *St John Passion*, with its dissonant oboes and

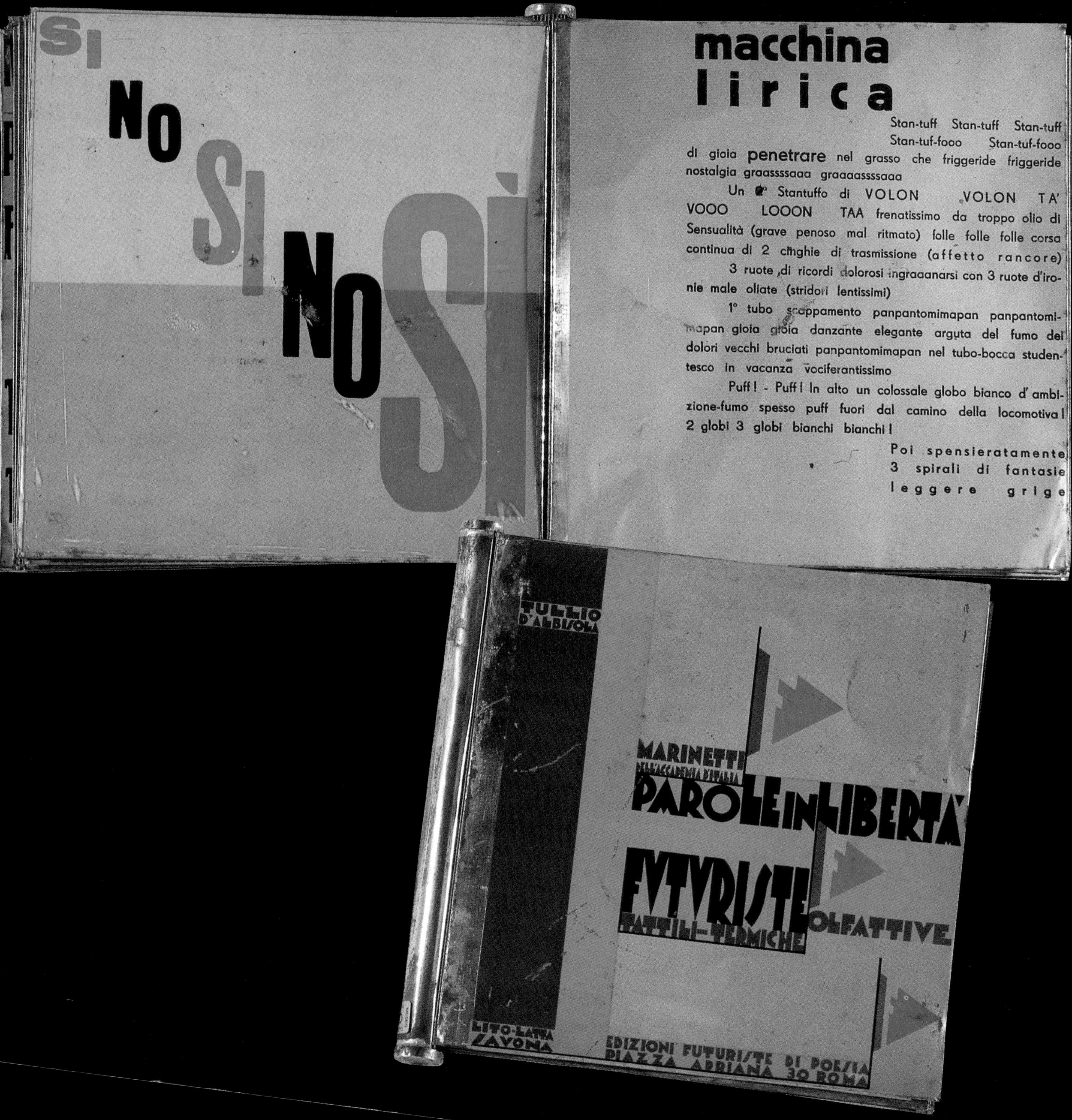

SI

NO SI NO SI

macchina
lirica

Stan-tuff Stan-tuff Stan-tuff
Stan-tuf-fooo   Stan-tuf-fooo
di gioia **penetrare** nel grasso che friggeride friggeride
nostalgia graassssaaa graaaassssaaa

Un Stantuffo di VOLON   VOLON TA'
VOOO   LOOON   TAA frenatissimo da troppo olio di
Sensualità (grave penoso mal ritmato) folle folle folle corsa
continua di 2 cinghie di trasmissione (affetto rancore)

3 ruote di ricordi dolorosi ingraaanarsi con 3 ruote d'iro-
nie male oliate (stridori lentissimi)

1° tubo scappamento panpantomimapan panpantomimapan gioia gioia danzante elegante arguta del fumo dei
dolori vecchi bruciati panpantomimapan nel tubo-bocca studen-
tesco in vacanza vociferantissimo

Puff! - Puff! In alto un colossale globo bianco d'ambi-
zione-fumo spesso puff fuori dal camino della locomotiva!
2 globi 3 globi bianchi bianchi!

Poi spensieratamente
3 spirali di fantasie
leggere   grige

TULLIO D'ALBISOLA

MARINETTI
DELL'ACCADEMIA D'ITALIA

PAROLE IN LIBERTA'

FUTURISTE

TATTILI-TERMICHE   OLFATTIVE

LITO-LATTA
SAVONA

EDIZIONI FUTURISTE DI POESIA
PIAZZA ADRIANA 30 ROMA

flutes, it is only in America that the railroad is properly represented in the pages of the musical score. Some draw a comparison between the pronounced beat of gospel music and the rhythm of a locomotive.

Each of the private railroad companies of the Confederation had its own hymn exalting the mythology of the train, and the songs about Casey Jones, the engine driver, and of the hobos in the freight cars, have become part of popular American tradition. There is a clear reference to the train in the *Grand Canyon Suite*, composed in the thirties by Ferde Grofé, the versatile and talented first violinist of Paul Whiteman's orchestra, with the echo of the shrill, atonal whistle of the Southwest Chief, that famous train running between Chicago and

Futurism's view of the railways. This early twentieth-century avant-garde movement achieved a happy symbiosis of art, power and speed. *Below:* A 1928 poster by Cassandre, inspired by the train. *Opposite:* The cover and two inside pages of the tin book by Tullio d'Albisola (1931).

Los Angeles which was the favourite of the Hollywood film goddesses.

However, the most memorable work on the railway theme is unquestionably *Pacific 231* by Arthur Honegger, a piece described, in the baroque manner, as a "chorale," which for some ten minutes reproduces with absolute naturalism the sound of a moving locomotive, quite without the orchestral colouring and emotional content which is usually present in a symphony. Honegger was originally an impressionistic composer, then came to be influenced by Stravinsky and finally became a polytonalist. He was born in Le Havre, the port and railway terminus of the line running along the Seine. His composition was a tribute to the marvels of industry and progress during the immediate postwar years, a theme underlined by the obsessive rhythms. He celebrated anew the line, so dear to Monet in his paintings *Gare de St Lazare* and *Pont d'Argenteuil*, which followed the winding course of the great river. The Pacific 231 locomotive, incidentally, was part of the imposing stock, manufactured in America, 200 of which were commissioned by the Soviet government for Lenin's 50th birthday.

Darius Milhaud wrote the music for the ballet *Le train bleu*, a reference to the famous train which ran right through France from Calais to the Côte d'Azur, of which a remnant was on show until a few years ago on a dead line at San Remo station, on the Italian Riviera. Celebrated artists, all of whom helped to break or alter accepted aesthetic canons, collaborated on the ballet: Diaghilev did the choreography, Cocteau the book, Picasso the scenery and Coco Chanel the costumes. Nor should we forget certain specific cadences in the works of Bela Bartok.

On a more frivolous note, it is worth mentioning the *Ballo Excelsior* by Romualdo Marenco, composed in honour of the Fréjus; *Take the A Train*, the Harlem train, which became the theme song of the great Duke Ellington; and the boogie *Honky-tonky Train Blues* by Meade Lux Levis, celebrating the arrival at New Orleans of The River Cities train from Mississippi, now running from St Louis.

From America, too, came *Chatanooga Choo Choo*, on the theme of the train that travelled over the Alleghenies and through the Tennessee Valley, associated with the victories of General Grant in the Civil War and with Roosevelt's New Deal of the thirties. It was particularly popular at the end

Opposite: Rain, Steam and Speed (1844) by Joseph Mallord William Turner.

Above: Gare de Saint-Lazare by Claude Monet, painted in 1877. The bridges, the steam from the locomotives, the metal framework and the chiaroscuro effects are all elements that lend modernity and realism to this famous work.

of the Second World War, its rhythm as familiar as that of the equally popular *In the Mood* in August 1945.

THE IMAGE OF SPEED

The fundamental invention of the photographic printing process – a plate impregnated with silver chloride, treated after exposure of the subject to the fumes of iodine and mercury – occurred at almost the same time as the birth of the railway. Daguerre and Stephenson both lived in the early nineteenth century, though on opposite sides of the Channel. Early photographers were confronted with the obvious practical difficulties of reproducing the moving train.

The photographs of American Civil War troop trains, taken by Matthew Brady, were particularly in demand; those of Alfred Stieglitz, the German-born American engineer and founder of the Photo Secession group in New York, were also important. One of them, from 1902, *The Hand of Man*, shows a train in perspective, rails glittering and thick smoke belching from the locomotive which is silhouetted against the light and shade of the cloudy sky, in the grey Pennsylvania dawn.

Half a century later, in 1955, the swansong of the steam locomotive was commemorated in a masterly surrealistic photograph by the Kansas-born Eugene Smith, previously the official photo reporter of *Life* during the Second World War. It shows a lean-faced railroad worker busy extinguishing glowing brands from the engine's firebox which have fallen on to the track.

In the course of the century, some of the great names in photography, notably

Nadar and Cartier-Bresson, had at some stage of their careers taken unforgettable shots of trains and railways.

The task of the painter who decides to capture on canvas the image of speed is far less straightforward. Obviously, as a result of railways having developed in the British Isles, English painters pointed the way. The Tate Gallery in London houses *Rain, Steam and Speed*, painted in 1844 by William Turner, which is a prototype of the genre. In the same vein, the undervalued painter William Frith painted *The Railway Station at Egham*, now in a private collection.

Later the Impressionists and Symbolists were to discover the fascination of locomotives and carriages, particularly Monet with *Un train dans la campagne*, which dates from the time of the defeat of Sédan, and then with *La gare de St Lazare*, one of the masterpieces of Impressionist art. In the same category are Sisley – in one of his notebooks there is a sketch of some clouds of steam – and Pissarro with *Le chemin de fer de Dieppe*.

For the Futurists the train was certainly a powerful machine, capable of generating ever-increasing energy and speed, truly the transport method of the future. No wonder, therefore, that they devoted special attention to it. Marinetti, although not a painter, had flashes of inspired vision: the greedy stations devouring the smoking serpents, the broad-chested locomotives pawing at the rails like huge steel horses harnessed with tubes.

The list continues with Kadinsky, who painted *Railway at Murnau*; Goncharova, with *Small Station* (Astapovo, where Tolstoy died); and Carrà, with *La stazione di Milano*.

Salvador Dalì, in the *Mystique de la gare*

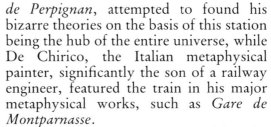

*B*elow: Boccione with Marinetti, founder of Futurism.

Right: Treno in velocità (Train at high speed) by Ivo Pannaggi (1922).

Opposite: Stati d'animo I: gli addii (States of mind I: farewells) by Umberto Boccioni (1911).

de Perpignan, attempted to found his bizarre theories on the basis of this station being the hub of the entire universe, while De Chirico, the Italian metaphysical painter, significantly the son of a railway engineer, featured the train in his major metaphysical works, such as *Gare de Montparnasse*.

Other painters who have treated the subject include Magritte, with *La durée poignardée* and his models of trucks, the Americans Charles Sheeler and Edward Hopper, the German Georg Scholz, and the Czechoslovakian Josef Sima, with his tubular train crossing a bridge over the Vltava.

65

THE SCREEN VERSION

The story of the cinema began on 28 December 1895, when there was a showing, in the cellar of the Gran Café on the Boulevard des Capucines in Paris, of a train arriving at the station of Besançon, birthplace of the Lumière brothers. The unusual spectacle at first caused puzzlement, then disquiet and finally alarm, for the puffing locomotive seemed about to burst out at the spectators from the huge white screen. Be that as it may, there was already common ground between railway and film.

In a way it was a deliberate choice. Cinema, like the train, is all about movement, drama, emotion, perspective and space. The enigmatic beauty of Marlene Dietrich's face is as closely associated with the steamed-up train window in *Shanghai Express* as it is with the dramatic *Blue Angel*, both directed by Joseph von Sternberg. No one can forget Greta Garbo's poignantly sorrowful expression prior to her suicide at the station in *Anna Karenina*.

It is impossible to list all the films in which the train has appeared as the central or, failing that, the main supporting contributor to the events depicted. So a brief and rapid survey of some of the most important and memorable instances must suffice.

The Italian actor Totò donned the uniform of a stationmaster in *Destinazione Piovarolo*, but the Italian masterpiece among railway films is still Pietro Germi's *Il ferroviere*. And in *Stazione Termini*, Vittorio de Sica told the story, against a railway background, of two secret lovers, played by Montgomery Clift and Jennifer Jones.

Railways in wartime are of course prominently featured on the screen. No-

Below: A shot of Pietro Germi in the film *Il ferroviere* (The Railwayman), a neorealist masterpiece set in Rome in the 1950s.
Opposite: Montgomery Clift on the set of *Stazione Termini*.

table French examples include René Clement's *La bataille du rail*, an epic of life and work on the railway, played by non-professional actors, some of whom had actually experienced the events shown on the screen. In *Le train*, by Pierre Granier-Deferre, set in occupied France, a man played by Jean-Louis Trintignant meets a Jewish refugee (Romy Schneider) on the train to La Rochelle, and provides her with false papers. At a police checkpoint the woman pretends not to know her benefactor so as not to involve him, while he cannot repress a gesture of tenderness which betrays him. Edward Fox, however, in *Day of the Jackal*, sent by the OAS to assassinate De Gaulle in Paris, which he reaches on a local train, manages to escape the road block set up by police as he makes his getaway. The timeless *Brief Encounter*, starring Celia Johnson and Trevor Howard, is one of the most famous railway films ever made.

A much more light-hearted film was *Le plaisir* by Max Ophüls, with a final episode (*La maison Tellier*) taking place in a train compartment. Zola's *La bête humaine* was also successfully translated on to the big screen.

In the United States, too, the cinema made its debut with a railway subject, in this case *The Great Train Robbery*. The attack on a train was to be a classic and almost obligatory feature of many Westerns, endlessly repeated, with now and then a few colourful variations, as in the Mexican setting of *Viva Villa*. Another recurring theme was the duel on the car roof, in which the gunmen providentially lowered their heads or threw themselves flat at the approach of the inevitable tunnel.

More modest in scale, and so slow and deliberate in pace as to build up an almost

unbearable tension, was Fred Zinnemann's classic Western *High Noon*, in which the climax is the arrival of the train carrying the vengeful killer at the station of the small town where the sheriff (Gary Cooper) waits for the final shootout. In Cecil B. de Mille's *The Greatest Show on Earth*, the highlight is the scene of the circus train being derailed and plunging over a precipice, one of the most sensational filmed sequences of an accident. De Mille also directed *Giant's Way*, an epic, made in the thirties, of the Union Pacific coast-to-coast railroad, with Barbara Stanwyck and Joel McCrea, a subject later treated by the Italian director Sergio Leone in his masterpiece, *Once Upon a Time in the West*.

The great American silent comedian, Buster Keaton, master of nonsense and improbability, in 1923 had a railway line built, complete with an 1840 train, for *Our Hospitality*, which provided the inspiration, three years later, for *The General*, a masterpiece of the silent cinema, set during the Civil War, in which he drives the locomotive of that name safely through the enemy lines. The Marx Brothers, too, were involved with trains in *Go West*, the title taken from the inscription on the cars sacrificed as firewood for the locomotive: a symbolic sequence, as with ships, of the train which consumes itself.

In a wholly different vein was Edward Sutherland's *Diamond Jim*, placidly played by Edward Arnold, here the inventor and builder of railway cars who, in order to demonstrate the superiority of his materials, arranges a head-on collision between two trains – empty, obviously.

It is interesting to note that the "red light" legend goes back to the early days of the railroads, to Carson City, where the freight trains stopped over for the night.

Opposite: A still from the film *Lady L.*, with Sophia Loren, David Niven and Paul Newman, shot at Monte Carlo in January 1965. The train from a bygone period contrasts with the skyscrapers already going up in the tiny principality. The station of Monte Carlo was later demolished and trains sent through a tunnel to allow this priceless stretch of coastline to be exploited by property developers.
Above: Totò in the film *Destinazione Piovarolo*.

The brakemen, who carried a red lamp as part of their outfit in the cabins, often took them along on their visits to local brothels and hung them outside the doors. It was then the job of the stationmaster to hunt the men out from the haunts where the red lights flickered so that the trains could be on their way.

Naturally other countries, too, have provided the setting for railway film sub-jects, from the small Irish station in *The Quiet Man*, where the final scene is shot, to the non-existent train, half-buried in the Amazon rainforest, in Herzog's *Fitzcarraldo*. Russia is featured in Kukhrai's *Ballad of a Soldier* and *Doctor Zhivago*, India in *Gandhi* and *A Passage to India*.

Among thrillers which feature trains are Hitchcock's *The Lady Vanishes*, and the film version of Agatha Christie's *Murder*

Below: Buster Keaton in *The General*.

on the Orient Express. Most of the war and disaster films are far less accomplished – an exception being Frankenheimer's *The Train*, concerning the attempted theft of works of art by the Nazis in occupied France – including potboilers of the caliber of *The Cassandra Crossing*, *Avalanche Express* and *Von Ryan's Express*, certain to appeal to those who are familiar with the European railway system.

The train continues to play a leading role in more recent films, such as *Out of Africa*.

This is a sure sign that the subject pleases the general public and that it retains its popularity even with those who do not normally travel by train. The automobile companies themselves often choose exotic railway settings for their publicity shots. And considering the wide diffusion nowadays of video-recorders, it is well worth capturing railway scenes on film. In a few years cinephiles may come to regard them as precious rarities.

A scene from *Murder on the Orient Express* and the initials of the Venice Simplon Orient Express company which restored the famous train.
On the following pages: A shot from *Once Upon a Time In The West* by Sergio Leone.

CHAPTER 3

WAR AND PEACE

The locomotive remains the very stuff of our childhood dreams but it is less happily associated, too, with images of war, where it has played a central role as it has always done in peacetime. Accustomed as we have become to an extended period of peace, a military train now seems singularly unsuited to be linked to an electric locomotive.

During the Second World War the train was used to ferry countless victims of the Holocaust to their death in concentration camps. The Burma railway is a further tragic example that claimed so many lives during these sad years. Trains at this time were often laden with human cargo – troops en route to a distant battlefield or innocent civilians destined for evacuation, deportation or imprisonment.

The Ringbahn in Berlin, a city that has always been heavily reliant on the railways, was the last bastion against the Soviet advance in April 1945; today many stretches of track, which have never been repaired, remain, overgrown by grass, as a reminder of the events that took place during that bleak period in twentieth-century history. Prior to this, Berlin station was the frequent setting for formal red-carpet state welcomes to visiting heads of state, but as the Second World War came to be dominated by air power, all this officialdom came to an end. The railway network fed the army's supply lines and, as soon as ground was recovered from the enemy, the sappers would be busy rebuilding bridges and replacing the ripped-up tracks. From the vehicle of potentates and conquerors, the train thus became an instrument of war. More recently, surrendering this belligerent role, it has come to be a target of revolutionaries, terrorists and insurrectionists.

Electrification of the railways has to a certain extent robbed the train of its most lingering, evocative image, associated with its origins, of the grimy locomotive, with billowing steam and screeching silver wheels. Much of the magic of a former age can, however, be relived by aficionados when one of these old machines is dragged out of a dark shed, polished, decked out in splendour and used to haul a special train, usually to mark some commemorative occasion. This is the train at its glorious best.

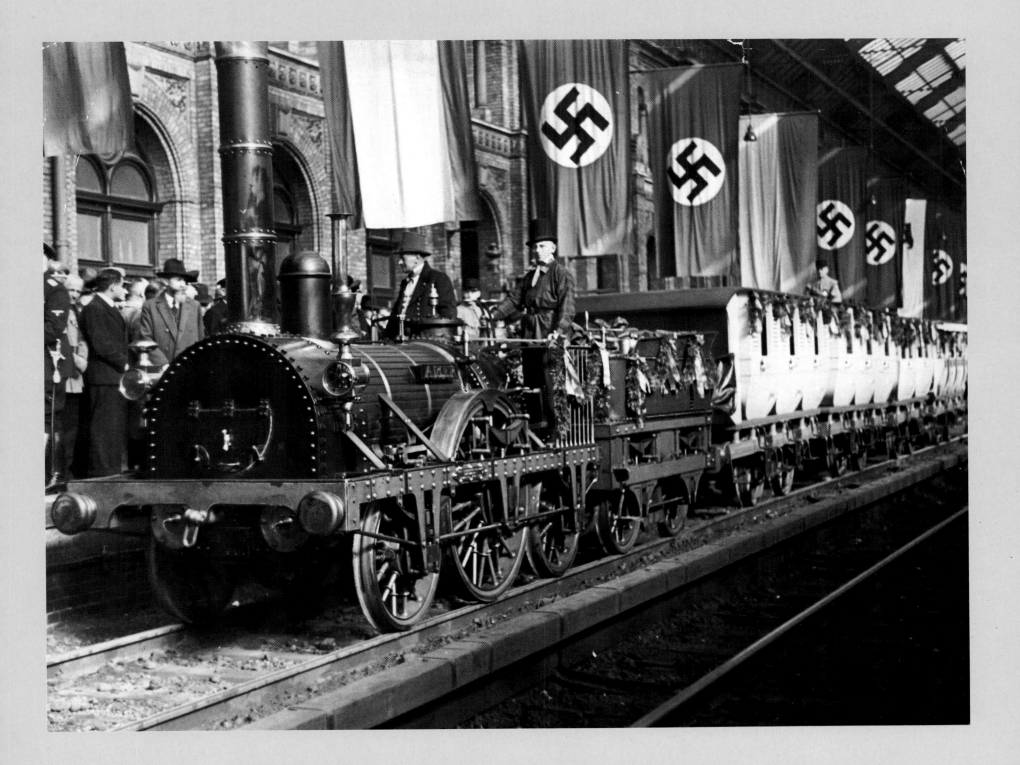

A NEW WAY OF GOING TO WAR

In its early days the Liverpool and Manchester Railway in England conveyed a regiment of soldiers over a distance of 43 miles (54.7 km) in two hours. It would have taken two days to cover the same distance on foot. Had there been a railway in 1815 the Battle of Waterloo might have been less of a "close run thing" by speeding the advance of Marshal Blücher to the help of the Duke of Wellington. The lesson was absorbed by the military establishment and in due course the use of railways in war was seriously debated. In 1859 a British periodical commented that the railways were: "a means ready to hand for conversion from mercantile purposes to engines of war." Soon afterwards an anonymous staff officer wrote to the London *Times* that a cordon of armoured trains might surround London. Ordnance could be mounted on armour-plated trucks and the locomotives could be protected by "shot-proof shields." Another military man suggested "portable batteries as a means of 'concentrating with unerring certainty a crushing force of artillery, with guns of heavier caliber than even the warships of the invader could command.'" He quoted trials which had shown that a gun of 81 tons (82.3 tonnes) could be moved and fought on the railway.

Some of these ideas were put to use in the American Civil War of 1861–65 when armour-plated gun-carrying trucks were used for the first time in modern warfare. Protection was by means of heavy timber with rails spiked to them. A gun from a field battery was mounted on the truck and fired through a porthole at the front. Slits for musketry fire were pierced in the side walls. Trains of this kind were propelled by a locomotive at the rear which at first was

unprotected because it was thought that the wagons ahead would form an efficient screen. In practice the locomotives proved highly vulnerable to flying bullets and the crew often had to lie on the floor of the cab to escape injury. Later in the war the cabs were armour-plated.

Four armour-plated wagons carrying guns were used by the French during the Franco-Prussian war. The plating was 2 in (50.8 mm) thick and field gun shells did no more than dent it. The locomotive was similarly protected. Two armour-plated gun trucks, each carrying two machine guns, were used by the British Army during the campaign in Egypt in 1882. Protection was by iron plating and sandbags. A wagon was also used to transport a 9-pounder gun but this was unshipped before it was fired, a crane being fitted to the wagon for this purpose. Five armoured trains carrying 6 in (154.2 mm) and 9.2 in (233 mm) guns were built by the British for use in the South African campaign of 1899–1902.

In modern warfare the tank and the armoured fighting vehicle have supplemented the armoured train and score over it in speed and mobility. The role of the railways in transporting men and supplies has, however, remained of paramount importance. In the outbreak of war in 1914 both Germany and Russia had "strategic" timetables already prepared and put them into operation. In the opening fortnight of war in 1914 a freight train crossed the Rhine Bridge at Cologne once every ten minutes. The Russian railways did not do so well. The lines in the west had been starved of equipment while resources were poured into the routes into Siberia and Central Asia which had been seen as of greater strategic importance. In trying to restore the balance the government was frustrated by Russian manufacturers demanding excessive prices for their products. Orders were therefore placed in the United States for 1,000 locomotives and 30,000 wagons while attempts were made to recruit staff from the same source. But the effort was too late and soon the Russian war effort crumbled under the impact of revolution at home. In the civil war which followed, the railways became targets for both sides and traffic was constantly disrupted by the destruction of lines and bridges.

In both world wars the railways in Britain were heavily involved in the movement of men and equipment to the Channel ports and in the evacuation of wounded and refugees. After the capture of Ostend by the Germans in October 1914, 26,000 Belgians passed through Dover or Folkestone in one week. The Marine station at Dover was in course of reconstruction before the war but the work had not been finished. A massive effort was then made. All available labour was commandeered and by working day and night the station was made fit for transferring the wounded from ship to train in ten days.

At the outbreak of war all the railways in Britain had come under government control and were managed by a Railway Executive Committee to which the general managers of the various companies were appointed. At once the War Office gave the railways 60 hours in which to assemble the locomotives and rolling stock necessary to convey the Expeditionary Force to Southampton. All was, in fact, ready in 48 hours and between 4 August and the end of the month 711 trains carried troops and material to the port, all converging on the London and South Western Railway. The load on the LSWR, which had begun in 1838 as the London and Southampton

Opposite and above: Prints from the Boer War. The train was involved in many actions and control of the railways became strategically indispensable as fighting between the Boers and the British developed.

Railway, was prodigious. Traffic was most intensive on 22 August when eight trains arrived between 6.12 and 7.36 a.m., another eight between 12.12 and 1.36 p.m., and 21 in the four hours between 2.12 and 6.12 p.m. All the railways were praised by Lord Kitchener in his first speech as Minister of State for War when he said: "The railway companies in the all-important matter of the transport facilities, have more than justified the confidence placed in them by the War Office, all grades of railway services having laboured with untiring energy and patience."

There were no fewer than 176 military camps on the LSWR system and throughout the war the leave traffic at weekends put a heavy load on the railway's resources. It was found that an average of 16,500 men travelled either on Friday evening or Saturday morning, requiring about 21 special trains. There had to be quick response to unforeseen circumstances. The 33 transports bringing the first contingent of troops from Canada were scheduled to arrive at Southampton but at the last moment were diverted to Plymouth. The men had to be conveyed to camps on Salisbury Plain, and arrangements had to be hastily revised to provide the 92 trains necessary to convey them and to assemble them at the South Western's Plymouth Friary or Devonport stations.

The railway companies' ships were also taken over by the government when hostilities began. Out of 126 acquired, 31 were lost by enemy action or accident attributable to war conditions. The cargo steamer *Guernsey* was wrecked on the French coast because the light at Cap de la Hogue had been extinguished as a security measure. Four of the losses were in the LSWR fleet. The *Normandy* and the *South Western* were torpedoed while on regular passenger services. The *Sarnia* was converted into an armed boarding vessel and while on these duties was sunk by an enemy torpedo. The fourth vessel was the *Guernsey* whose loss on the French coast is recorded above.

Vessels of all the railways were converted into hospital ships. The Brighton company's *Sussex* was torpedoed on the run from Folkestone to Dieppe. Although the forepart was blown off it was possible to beach her. The ship was then requisitioned by the French Government and taken to Le Havre where she was repaired and returned to service.

While the lines in the South bore the brunt of the traffic to the Channel ports, all the others carried unprecedented traffic. The resources of the smaller companies were sometimes overtaxed but the centralized management by the Railway Executive Committee enabled locomotives and rolling stock to be deployed where required. Locomotives had to be loaned to the Highland Railway which was called upon to run many specials over its remote northern section to Thurso to provision the fleet at Scapa Flow. They were known as "Jellicoe Specials" after the Admiral of the Fleet.

Inevitably the exceptional traffic and operating conditions of wartime heightened the risk of accidents and it is a tribute to the railway staff that so few could be attributed to these circumstances. The most disastrous incident in the First World War had its origin in unauthorized procedures by the two signalmen working the box at Quintinshill, north of Carlisle. They were supposed to change shifts at 6 a.m. but it was more convenient for the day man to come on duty at 6.30 because he could then get a lift on a local train. The man on the night shift agreed to wait for him and after 6 a.m. he recorded train movements on a

CHEMIN DE FER DU NORD
NEDERLANDSCHE SPOORWEGEN
SOCIÉTÉ NATIONALE DES CHEMINS DE FER BELGES
ÉTOILE DU NORD
AU DÎNER
AU DÉJEUNER
PULLMAN
PARIS—BRUXELLES—AMSTERDAM
COMPAGNIE DES WAGONS-LITS

Left: A publicity poster from the thirties for L'Etoile du Nord, the famous Paris–Brussels–Amsterdam express which ran through territory repeatedly contested by France and Germany. The long period of tension between the two powers erupted in the three bloody wars of 1870–71, 1914–18 and 1939–45, and involved the use of armoured trains. Millions died to win the few dozen miles of ground between Alsace and Lorraine.
Above: A scene from René Clement's film *Bataille du Rail*, dealing with the French Resistance during the Second World War.

sheet of paper instead of entering them in the signalbox register. The day man on arrival at the box copied these entries into the book so that when the book was inspected the change in handwriting would be seen at the official time for the change of shift.

When the day man arrived he had intended to move the local train into a loop off the northbound main line to leave the way clear for expresses heading towards Glasgow. On this occasion he could not do so because the loop was occupied by a goods train. He therefore shunted it across to the southbound main line. This was a safe procedure, which had been followed before, providing the rules were observed. On this occasion, however, the man seems to have been paying more attention to writing up the register and chatting with his colleague, who had stayed on to read the war news. By this time an empty coal train had arrived in the loop on the southbound side of the line and the crews of both trains had come into the box.

Apparently without realizing what he was doing, the signalman inexplicably "ac-

Two types of rail vehicle used in war.

Above and below right: Front and side view of the Sumida M. 2593 armoured car, used by the Japanese in Manchuria.

Below left: The "Dictator," a 13-inch motorized mortar used by the Northern army in the American Civil War.

cepted" a southbound troop train from the next box northward despite the fact that the parked local was standing in its path. A few minutes later the troop train collided at full speed with the local, which had its brakes full on and was virtually immovable. In the terrific impact the troop train was reduced to a heap of wreckage.

At this moment a northbound sleeping car express from Euston to Glasgow was approaching at speed. The signals were flung to danger, but too late to stop it. The express ploughed into the wreckage and collided with one of the engines involved in the earlier collision. The sudden stop telescoped the first three coaches. Wooden coaches with gas lighting and live coals from the wrecked locomotives led to the inevitable result. Fire broke out and raged for 24 hours.

Casualties among the officers and men of the Royal Scots Regiment on the troop train totalled 215 killed and 191 injured. The driver and fireman of the troop train were killed but apart from these there were only 10 civilian deaths. On the Euston–Glasgow express 51 passengers and 4

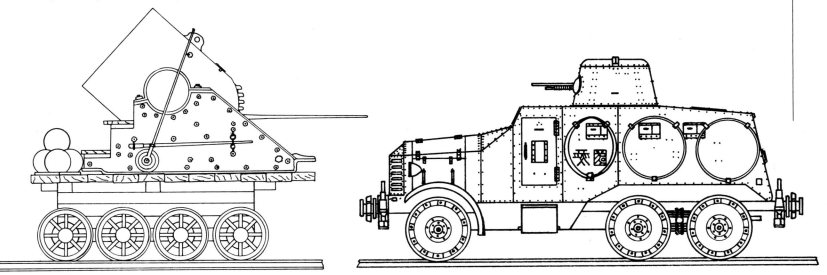

railway servants were seriously injured. It has never been possible to establish with certainty how many men on the troop train died because the Battalion Roll was lost. Only 52 survivors answered their names at a roll call in a field alongside the track after the accident.

The usual Ministry of Transport inquiry was held but the facts were not in doubt, although both signalmen denied sending the message that had brought the troop train to disaster. The inspecting officer found that inattention and failure to observe signalling procedures were the cause of the accident. It was ironic that the sleeping car train to Glasgow was running 30 minutes late. Had it been on time it would have passed Quintinshill in safety. Both signalmen were convicted of manslaughter and sentenced to imprisonment.

There are strict rules concerning the transport of munitions by train but certain accidents cannot be foreseen. On 18 April 1918 a goods train of the London, Brighton and South Coast Railway from Eastbourne was travelling through Redhill Tunnel when three wagons and the brake van broke away and were left in the tunnel. The signalman in the box ahead did not notice that the train was incomplete when it passed him and accepted a following goods train. It ran into the stationary wagons and wreckage blocked the tunnel. The fireman tried to get through the debris to give a

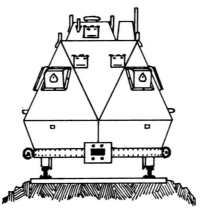

warning but as he struggled to do so he heard another train approaching from the direction of London and had to take cover. The train he heard was a special carrying munitions. It ran into the wreckage in its path and about 40 ft (12 m) of the tunnel were filled to the crown with smashed wagons and debris.

When the Second World War was seen to be inevitable in 1939 a Railway Executive Committee was again formed and provided with office space in a disused Underground station. Most of the headquarters offices of the individual railways were in London and during the first week in September they were evacuated, with all their equipment and files, to sites in the Home Counties. Emergency passenger timetables were issued in which main-line services were much reduced and top speed was limited to 60 mph (96 kmh) in order to reduce maintenance of rolling stock and track. By December 1939 an immediate onslaught on the country was judged to be unlikely. The speed limit was then raised to 70 mph (112.6 kmh) and some services were accelerated.

Early in 1940 the situation darkened and the early summer saw the evacuation from Dunkirk. Ordinary passenger services were reduced again and the remaining trains had to carry large numbers of service personnel. Train loads increased to far above normal. Some trains from Kings

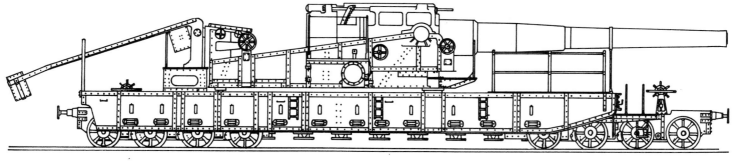

Cross to the North East and Scotland had to be lengthened on occasions to as many as 25 coaches.

Throughout the war the railways had to cope with shortage of personnel, materials, and plant required for maintenance. Railway works were fully occupied with manufacture of munitions, extended later to assembling aircraft parts, tanks and landing craft. After the blitz on Coventry on 14–15 November 1940 the city was virtually isolated from the rest of the railway system by 122 "incidents." A superlative effort by all concerned restored rail access to the city within a week.

Surprisingly there was some railway construction during the war. A number of new links and junctions were put in so that routes that had been damaged by bombing could be by-passed. The war had an effect on passenger services which can still be felt. Previously the principal expresses had not stopped at stations on the fringe of the outer suburban area. Travellers had to travel on a local service into London to join a main-line train, and similarly ride into London and out to their home station on returning. The blitz made it desirable to limit travel through London as far as possible. Additional stops were put in the schedule of long-distance trains so that passengers could alight and reach their home station without passing through a London terminus.

Some armoured rail vehicles.
Below: A 240-mm cannon built in France at the end of the nineteenth century.
Opposite below: A more powerful piece of French artillery used during the First World War; *above:* Front view of a German "panzer draisine," 1944.

When at length the invasion of Europe began the part played by the railways in launching and maintaining it was crucial, and they had to work under the continuous threat of "flying bombs" and rockets. In the four weeks after D-Day the flow of forces mail trains, ambulance trains, and trains bringing prisoners to camps in Britain added up to a total of 15,000 special services. It was a very war-weary railway system, unflatteringly described by one member of the post-war government as a poor bag of physical assets, that came under national ownership in 1945.

During the years between the wars bomber aircraft had increased in range, speed and bombload. With war apparently inevitable, plans were prepared to safeguard the civilian population, particularly children. In Britain during September 1939, 1,300,000 children were moved, half of them from London and the South-East, in nearly 4,000 special trains. Stations on the London Underground system were equipped as deep-level bomb shelters with bunks and other facilities. Eventually they could accommodate 75,000 people.

The evacuation of troops from Dunkirk faced the railways with a transport crisis that had not been foreseen and had to be tackled by hasty improvisation. The re-

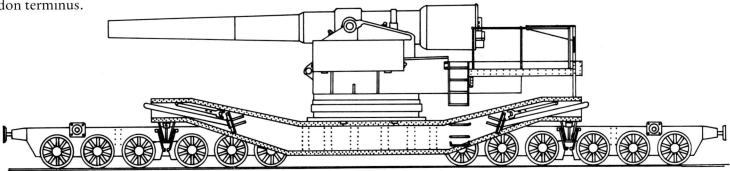

sponse was immediate. A total of 630 journeys were made and 319,000 men conveyed to destinations throughout the country.

Bombing by the Luftwaffe and later attacks by "flying bombs" and rockets inflicted far more serious damage on the railways than had been suffered in the First World War. In all, 4,000 carriages and wagons were destroyed, but only eight locomotives. Railwaymen stayed at their posts in conditions of great danger. Their courage was recognized by the award of three George Crosses and 29 George Medals.

When the time came for the invasion of Europe plans prepared in advance came into operation. Of the 54,000 trains run on the government's account between September 1939 and June 1945 more than half travelled in the last 18 months of the war.

On the Continent there were complex traffic flows as the outbreak of war approached. Events in France were recalled in newspaper and magazine articles 50 years later. Reservists were travelling to their units and holidaymakers were hurrying home to await what the future might bring. A public figure remembered how, as a boy of 15, he had been on holiday with his grandmother in Poland. His train home from Warsaw to Berlin was crowded with Polish soldiers on their way to the frontier. He had ten minutes for the connection to Paris by the last train to France. Luckily he arrived in Berlin on time. Otherwise he would have had to wait rather longer than ten minutes for the train home.

The authorities encouraged those who were able to leave Paris to do so. On 1 and 2 September an estimated 450,000 travellers took trains from the Gare St Lazare, Austerlitz, Montparnasse and the Gare de Lyon. The exodus was marred by a triple collision near Les Aubrais in which 33 lives were lost.

From the end of August more than 16,000 child evacuees left Paris for Dreux, Blois, Orléans and Nantes. Civilians in border zones and the families of military personnel were compulsorily evacuated. They hastily gathered the 66 lb (30 kg), which was all they were allowed, and set off for reception centers outside the danger zones. Some had uncomfortable journeys, crowded 50 or 60 at a time into freight wagons and finding on arrival at their destination that they were not expected. Elsewhere the arrangements were meticulous. In Strasbourg preparations had been made as early as April. On the appointed day 87,000 evacuees were conveyed in 78 trains to Périgueux, the 20-coach sets shuttling to and fro throughout the day. In

Below: Testing of an ambulance car in Washington, 7 October 1954. After the Korean War hospital trains took on an appearance very different to their First World War guise. More recent wars, fought in areas that often have no railways, have not provided many opportunities for such vehicles to go into service.

Opposite: An Italian poster commemorating the centenary of the German railway system in 1935.

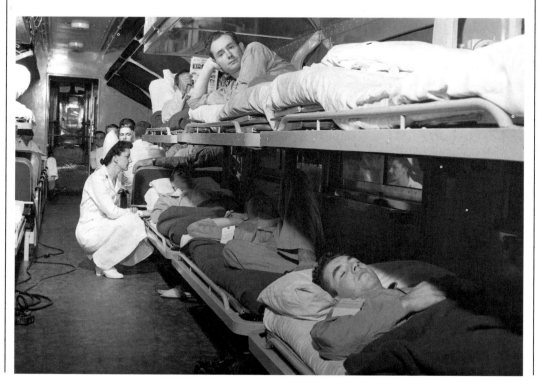

this area there were occasional fracas when German-speaking civilians encountered French troops. There was a lively scene at Paray-le-Monial when conscripts clashed with evacuees who had imprudently hung sheets decorated with swastikas in the windows of their carriage to dry. The soldiers tried to tear them down. The evacuees clung to their property and there was an outbreak of kicks and punches. Officers who hastened to quell the trouble were unable to do so and it was finally stopped by sounding the bugle for departure.

The state of war was reflected in locomotive design. In Great Britain, where elegance in contours and livery was traditional, an "austerity" locomotive put into service during the Second World War by the Southern Railway caused shocked surprise, by its gaunt appearance. It was, in fact, a boiler on wheels, stripped of all nonessentials. Later designs by the Ministry of Supply were similarly bleak but by that time austerity in its various manifestations had become familiar.

Germany produced three wartime designs (Kriegslokomotiven) developed for a pre-war freight locomotive. Over 8,000 were built between 1941 and 1945 to meet the ever-increasing demand for motive power in the occupied countries.

THE CARRIAGE AT COMPIÈGNE

The three great conflicts which pitted France against Germany between 1870 and 1945 helped to accelerate the expansion of the railway system in Europe. In 1844 – when trains were just beginning to make their mark – Helmut von Moltke, a Prussian general, realized that while France was discussing its military railways, Germany should be building them. This is exactly

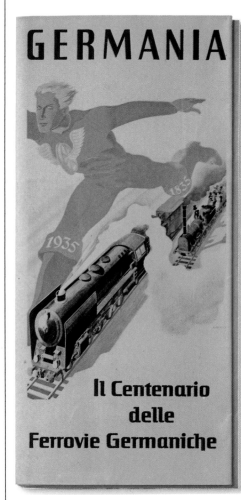

what happened. In 1859 he was on hand to witness the war between France and Austria, and later he would witness the part played by railways in the American Civil War.

In early August 1870 Germany began the much heralded advance on Paris which astonished and disturbed the world, given the speed of her mobilization and transport of half a million troops and their supplies, thanks to 1,200 trains. France, on the other hand, came up against all kinds of problems due to her disorganized rail network.

The Franco-Prussian war, in which military trains played a determining role, put an end to the second Napoleonic empire. Thereafter France set in motion the steps that were expected to contribute to her victory on the next occasion, which would find her much better prepared. Indeed the organization of the French railways was so efficient that the Germans were easily able to redeploy their troops after the battle of the Marne and to bring up the armoured train bearing the famous 420 cannon, the Big Bertha, directed at Paris.

Compiègne is a city in the department of the Oise, some 50 miles (80 km) from the capital, where in 1430 Joan of Arc was defeated and handed over to the English, and where in 1914 one of the bitterest battles of the First World War took place between the British and the Germans, effectively blocking the road to Paris. Today the famous Etoile du Nord (Paris–Amsterdam) and Parsifal (Paris–Cologne) expresses thunder past the forest where in 1918 the French supreme command was headquartered.

At five in the morning of Monday 11 November Marshal Foch handed over to Admiral Wemyss the harsh terms of surrender which subsequently formed the terms of the Treaty of Versailles. On a slab of stone beside the carriage the following words were inscribed in capital letters: "Here the criminal pride of the German empire surrendered, defeated by the free people it sought to enslave." It was a humiliation for Germany, not only for Hindenburg and the second Kaiser, but also for Bismarck and the first emperor who in 1871 had had himself proclaimed German Emperor in the Hall of Mirrors at Versailles.

In May 1940 a front of 310 miles (500 km) stretched from Basle to Montmédy. It was protected by the legendary and impregnable Maginot line. Turrets and platforms bristling with guns and antitank minefields stood above ground; below ground was a series of fortified towns, with living quarters, roads and a miniature railway system.

On the Friday before Whitsunday the

villagers of the Ardennes were in church celebrating the religious festival. At Euskirchen an armoured train arrived, carrying Hitler, a more modern version of the lord of darkness. His objective was Sedan – the famous site of France's decisive defeat in the Franco-Prussian war – and to this end he would violate for the second time Belgian neutrality, and outflank the mighty French fortification almost unopposed. This time the invasion would be successful, with German troops marching victoriously down the Champs Elysées.

"With a broken heart I have to tell you that we must stop fighting," sighed General Pétain, the veteran hero of Verdun, summoned to hold France until American reinforcements could come to their aid.

The Führer had already arranged for the old saloon-carriage of 1918 to be removed from the museum for a new armistice. He was to go there a few days later, seething with rage, contemptuous, bent on vengeance and eager for victory, almost as if the war had been launched with the sole aim of savouring this overwhelming moment of revenge. At 6.30p.m. on 22 June Hitler's envoys would set the seal, provisionally, on his triumph when the armistice was signed and three-fifths of France was surrendered to German control. Exactly a year later German armies invaded the Soviet Union – an offensive which led to Hitler's ultimate defeat.

On 25 August 1944, Dietrich von Choltitz, the last German commander of Paris, met General Leclerc at the Gare de Montparnasse to sign the act of surrender. He earned the hatred of a furious crowd but also the subsequent gratitude of future generations for having saved Paris – Ville Lumière – by refusing to obey the final order of the Führer. "Is Paris burning?" demanded the voice at the other end of the telephone. Von Choltitz did not reply.

The German general had not forgotten, however, to send a staff officer to destroy the fragile railway relic in the forest of Compiègne, following a direct despatch from Berlin. This was Hitler's final attempt to salvage some self-respect. He had been badly shaken by the assassination attempt a month earlier and was desperate to avoid the insult of another exit from the saloon-carriage. For him and his henchmen the Nuremberg noose was already being prepared. Only cyanide or a bullet through the head would enable them to escape it.

THE TRAIN AS LAST BASTION OF EMPIRE

Strategic military considerations have always determined governmental decisions, and to imagine that the train can be left out of such deliberations is mere wishful thinking. Thus the major railway projects of the past were often conceived either with a view to unifying a nation or to providing a means of control, a kind of bulwark for the defense of native soil.

The most striking example of this is the Trans-Siberian railway, which runs along the frontier of the Soviet Union. Historically, this was intended to restrain any expansionist moves by China, with its vast population, tempted perhaps by the unpopulated regions of the Far North. This was a genuine concern in Tsarist days and can be said to remain a source of anxiety even today among the present occupiers of the Kremlin. Nor is it only imperialist and one-party regimes that are confronted by such problems. Neutral Switzerland maintains its formidable Alpine security largely thanks to the Rhaetian Railways and the Furka-Overalp.

Opposite below: The indicator card for the Moscow–Zabaykal'sk car, the last station in the Soviet Union before the Chinese border in Manchuria. For many years the journey by Trans-Siberian express provided many visitors with a chance to test the mood of the two great Communist powers. Many special correspondents travelled on this line, particularly after the skirmishes on the Ussuri river in 1969 which threatened to flare up into full-scale war. The trains, however, continued to run between the two countries. However, gauge differences (in China the standard European gauge of 1,435 mm was operative whereas in the USSR the broader gauge of 1,524 mm applied) necessitated a change of bogie (above) to allow the trains to travel through directly.

These lines are the vital links for would-be defenders, with tunnels that could immediately be transformed into impregnable refuge places. This was well known to Switzerland when it proclaimed its neutrality on 1 September 1939 which it successfully preserved throughout the Second World War. It was equally understood by Hitler, who, taking into account the losses that the German army would doubtless suffer in order to reach the sources of the Rhine, decided not to invade.

In London there were endless discussions in Parliament and in the columns of *The Times* about the wisdom of building a tunnel under the Channel, which would inevitably have enabled an enemy army to emerge in the midst of the Kentish orchards. The fate of the Spanish and Portuguese railways was sealed when the monarchs of both countries made a joint decision to furnish their respective rail systems with a gauge 20cm wider than normal, in an attempt to avoid a repetition of the Napoleonic advance southward from the Pyrenees. The two nations had to wait almost a century for the brilliant invention of the engineers Goicochea and De Oriel – the Talgo trains with mobile trolleys capable of adapting to both gauges – to enable the Puerta del Sol to travel from Madrid to Paris without the unlucky passengers being ejected from their beds in the dead of night on arrival at Irun station.

In more recent times, however, the strategic function of the railways has appeared to become a thing of the past. Though perhaps ex-president Pinochet's plans to extend the railway line beyond the terminus of Puerto Montt was in fact a latent desire to colonize the extreme south of Chile and thus repel any Argentine claims. Recently the negotiations on nuclear arms limitation ran into trouble when the Amer-

icans learned that the Russians were planning to install intercontinental missiles on special railway trucks that could be moved at will, not subject to any control, from one end of the Urals to the other.

This strategy appeared almost impossible to neutralize, even with the aid of sophisticated spy satellites. It seems that the Pentagon then decided to imitate its rivals, and thus perhaps provide an opportunity for the United States to reorganize her railroads, worn by the movement of heavy goods trains.

THE NEMESIS OF HISTORY – VIOLENCE AND THE TRAIN

Political events and civil strife often hit railway services causing a suspension that may be temporary or, in more dramatic cases, semi-permanent. For example, there have been no direct trains between India and Bangladesh since the crisis of 1971, even though, according to those few bold individuals who have made the attempt, it is possible to cross the border by motor rickshaw and to catch the train on the other side. There is no such solution, however, from El Arish to Tel Aviv, in spite of the Camp David agreement and Egypt's desire to rebuild the Sinai line, destroyed during the Six-Day War. Since the surprise Israeli attack by Moshe Dayan's airforce in 1967 at the outbreak of the Arab-Israeli War, it has rusted beneath the desert sand.

The last train from Seoul to Pyongyang ran in 1950. Today South Korea's modern railcars proceed no farther than the town of Munsan. Just before reaching the Imjin river, which is the demarcation line between the two parts of the country, a huge locomotive stands in front of a large block of marble. A symbol of hope, it is always kept clean and shining, despite the ravages of time, so that one day it can resume its journey northward.

Once the principal instrument of nineteenth-century imperialism and colonial expansion, the train has sometimes become the victim of the very tensions which helped to bring it about. During the Second World War bombers began to make systematic attacks on bridges and junctions; and resistance groups continued to threaten the railways in order to disrupt the communications of the occupying forces. Attacks did not cease even when hostilities came to an end in 1945. When the smooth running of the railways has not been affected by political tensions between East and West or by the whims of local petty dictators, it has often been at the mercy of unscrupulous terrorists, who have targeted trains and stations alike for the sake of their causes.

On Saturday 2 August 1980, the Ancona–Basle express stood on platform one at Bologna, Italy, full of holidaymakers returning from the Adriatic. In the hall other tourists and travellers, awaiting connections or the arrival of relatives and friends, milled around. Suddenly there was a tremendous explosion; the wing of the building was completely destroyed by a bomb concealed in a suitcase. In the rubble dozens lay dead and hundreds injured.

Why should bombers choose a train as a target for their evil exploits? Is it perhaps because they still identify the railway as the "long arm" of established government, and the train as the embodiment of the system they want to bring down? Or could it be just the reverse: that because the train has become an increasingly popular vehicle, it invites the hatred of those who wish to terrorize people for supporting a form of progress engineered by those in power?

The Korean War (1950–53), with its continual shifts of front and massive bombardments, inflicted serious damage to that country's rail network. After establishing a precarious equilibrium, with the ceasefire at Panmunjon, the networks of North and South were rebuilt independently, with no point of contact.

Opposite: The central station of Seoul still retains its original architecture. From here air-conditioned trains leave every 15 minutes for Pusan, the country's second city and South Korea's principal port. The journey of 897 miles (1,445 km) takes just over four hours, with a couple of intermediate stops. North of the capital, however, the line suddenly comes to an end at Munsan, near the 38th parallel.

Below: A locomotive before a boundary stone, with an inscription that leaves no doubt as to the intentions of the South Koreans: "This train is longing to go North."

Whatever the reason, it is clear that the railway is especially vulnerable to the activities of saboteurs and also ordinary vandals. It is also true that it only needs a steel wedge between the rails to bring about a disaster of incalculable proportions.

Nevertheless, one of the principal advantages of rail travel, which often tends to be overlooked, is its safety. Although a train disaster, whether accidental or deliberate, may arouse a subconscious, irrational sense of fear, amplified by the normal media treatment, one forgets that road accidents, which happen almost every day, usually get no publicity, despite the fact that they have accounted for more fatalities than either world war.

PACTS AND AGREEMENTS

During the Second World War the Basque coast did not see many tourists. The grand hotels of Biarritz and St Jean de Luz were depressingly empty. In Paris the Nazi flag fluttered from the Eiffel Tower and Marshal Pétain had signed a humiliating armistice, safeguarding only a semblance of independence for the region known as "Free France." The Gascony coast was completely in the control of the Third Reich which, having failed to invade the British Isles, had begun to fortify the Atlantic shoreline.

One day, Hendaye station, close to the international bridge marking the border with Spain, swarmed with police and soldiers. Two mysterious, highly armed trains came to a halt side by side. The Führer had arrived from Berlin to meet Francisco Franco in person. Hitler was seeking repayment for the decisive contribution made by Germany in vanquishing the Republican army during the Spanish civil war that had ended barely a year before.

Not far away, across the frontier, lay Guernica station which had experienced the horrors of merciless blanket bombing at the hands of Goering's air force. On this occasion, however, the shrewd, impenetrable Galician general refused to join Hitler's alliance. Arguing that his country had not yet recovered from the terrible sufferings caused by the recent conflict, he declined the invitation to enter the European war on the side of the victorious Axis powers, promising merely to make a symbolic gesture by sending Spanish volunteers, the Blue Division later despatched to the Ukraine in the "crusade" against the Bolsheviks.

Hitler, furious, boarded the train again,

The interior of the station at Hendaye, the last French town before the Spanish border on the Basque coast. Here, in 1940, Adolf Hitler tried in vain to persuade Franco to enter the war on the side of the Axis. On the square outside is a smaller station which is the departure point of the electric train for San Sebastian, known as El Topo. This is the first stretch of the longest narrow-gauge line to be found in Europe. The Cornice Cantabrica leads to El Ferrol, Franco's birthplace, in northern Galicia.

Opposite: A rare picture of the station at Hanoi, taken on 24 September 1945, the day on which French settlers made their temporary return after the years of Japanese occupation.

silently cursing the ungrateful Spaniard who dared to spurn his offer of an alliance. "I would rather have all my teeth pulled than return to Hendaye," he was to reply later when advised to make a new approach. In the remaining 35 years of his life, Franco must have had many reasons to congratulate himself on his steadfast attitude on that day at the Basque station.

The 1940 railway encounters between Hitler and Mussolini, with their respective entourages, at the Brenner Pass, had a completely different outcome. Here the station platform and the official trains were the setting for the fatal pact which was to have tragic consequences for Mussolini.

More recently, the train, though superseded by the airplane as the principal means of transporting the world's leaders to high-level conferences, has continued to provide the backdrop to many historic meetings for the signing of pacts and peace agreements. In 1974, for example, America's President Ford visited Anwar Sadat in Egypt travelling by official train from Cairo to Alexandria. His warm reception by crowds reinforced his determination to regain American diplomatic supremacy in the Arab world which was increasingly being wooed by the Soviet Union.

The meetings which sought reconciliation between Zambia and Rhodesia — which had not yet become independent Zimbabwe — took place in a railway carriage stationed on the international Livingstone Bridge above the Victoria Falls. The train had stopped precisely at the demarcation line between the two countries so that the respective diplomats could come to the treaty table without venturing outside their own territory.

Openings of new lines have certainly provided ideal occasions for high-sounding speeches about peace and concord among nations, to the accompaniment of waving flags and solemn fanfares. The ceremonies marking the inauguration of the great transalpine tunnels were just such opportunities. Unhappily, these moving words were destined to be negated within a few years by the roar of guns.

This is not always true. In certain rare instances the guns have ceased firing for good, paving the way for a long period of cooperation and prosperity. In Scandin-avia, for example, there were bloody wars until the nineteenth century. At Magnor, the Norwegian frontier station on the Stockholm–Oslo line, a monument was erected by the pacifists of both nations with a promise never to take up arms against each other. It is a pity that nobody sees it. Most of the tourists pass through Magnor in their wagons-lits in the middle of the night.

CHAPTER 4

THE GREAT TRAINS

All trains are distinguished by a number. This figure, however, is a cold, anonymous form of identification which is difficult even for those employed by the railways to remember. So the most important trains also bear a name. Many of them are virtually part of the everyday language, such as the Orient Express or the Blue Train. If we have selected only a few here, it is simply because there are so many to choose from.

Naturally each country has its own preference as to how to label its engines. In France every new locomotive emerging from the workshop is given the name of a city, much as other nations do in the case of their airliners and ships. The inauguration ceremony itself takes on a special significance: the locomotive is driven to the town after which it is named, and in the presence of political and local dignitaries is furnished with a plate bearing the city's insignia.

Almost every nation concurs in giving special names to its most important trains. Cook's Continental Timetable lists more than 40 named international expresses. The Americans honour the memory of famous statesmen such as Benjamin Franklin or Thomas Jefferson in naming their Atlantic coast trains. The numerous freight trains that run day and night in all kinds of weather all over the United States have also acquired names and nicknames. Often these names reflect something of the colour and romance of American railroading. Sometimes they relate to the railroad's history, the area served by the railroad or the nature of the railroad's services: Cannonballs, Bullets, Rockets, Meteors, Thunderbolts and Redballs. These are names with the flavour of speed and the roar of the rails. There are colourful animal nicknames: Badger, Bulldog, Blackcat, Whippet and Greyhound. A train carrying fresh vegetables and fruits on an overnight special train might bear the name of Vegetable Special. They also bear the names of cities, states and other geographical areas.

The Japanese choose poetic names like Cherry Flower or Morning Breeze – unfortunately lost on Western tourists because they are inscribed in Japanese script.

In general, however, the name of a train, when wisely chosen, adds allure to the journey. Sometimes it may even create a legend.

PERSEUS

In England the Eastern Region, operating between London and the industrial North and North-East of the country, introduced a series of fast trains morning and evening, tailored to the needs of businessmen, who could buy inclusive tickets covering the fare, seat reservation, and meals in the restaurant car. Anticipating a trend, the region probably flattered its clientele by adding the word "Executive" to the description of the train leading to the creation of such services as The Hull Executive, The Cleveland Executive and so on.

Fast trains on lines which were not electrified were hauled at first by diesel locomotives but from 1976 onwards they began to be formed of sets of seven or eight permanently coupled coaches with a diesel power car at each end. The power cars were designed for this particular duty and could not be used in general traffic like a locomotive. At first these trains were known as High Speed Trains (HSTs) but as they were designed for a top speed of 125 mph (201 kmh) they were given the collective name InterCity 125, although the more convenient contraction HST continues to be used except in British Railways publicity. Individual services carried names, as some of them had done in the past. From then on British Railways resumed the practice of naming trains on quite a large scale, keeping the famous old ones alive and inventing others. Unfortunately the former practice of carrying nameboards at roof level had to be dropped because of the intensive use of the rolling stock and the labour of removing the boards from an HST on arrival because the same set of coaches would soon leave again on a service with another name or no name at all.

Certain InterCity services are described as Pullman. They are no longer composed of special rolling stock throughout as in the

BRITISH RAILWAYS

Sacks of coal are loaded on to a wagon for the return journey of the Flying Scotsman steam locomotive, seen here at Twickenham, London, on 19 August 1969, before making a special run to Liverpool. Some five tons of coal are needed to fuel the powerful locomotive which still bears the insignia of the LNER, the private company which had been abolished 20 years previously under the Labour government's nationalization policy.
On the previous page: A close-up of the elegant Perseus Pullman car.
On the following pages: Typically Scottish scenes form the setting for a local Highland train. The poster celebrates another famous train, The Queen of Scots.

days of the Pullman Car Company, but the first-class coaches have been redecorated and the passenger enjoys a high-standard service of meals, drinks and refreshments at his seat with stewards on hand throughout the journey to minister to him as required.

InterCity spelled in that way is a trademark of British Railways and is used in some other countries. The German Federal Railway operates a network of fast services between important centres. The trains are designated "IC" and are timed to interconnect so that journeys over more than one IC route can be made with a single change of train and involve no more than crossing the platform at the interchange station. At first the IC trains were first class only but later second-class coaches were added.

Another brand name became familiar in Continental Europe when the railways joined forces to reply to air competition with a fleet of trains called Trans-Europe Expresses (TEE). Like the British HSTs, the first TEEs incorporated power cars instead of being hauled by locomotives. There were both diesel and electric versions, some of the latter designed for operating on different electrification systems. Services were individually named. The Gottardo between Zurich and Milan could work on all four main-line electrification systems in Europe. The TEEs were first class only and frontier stops were brief or replaced by customs formalities carried out on the train.

The TEEs were successful in attracting traffic, which in due course became so heavy that the original sets could not handle it and trains of locomotive-hauled coaches had to be substituted. The first of these came into operation between Paris, Brussels and Amsterdam in 1964. After 1979 none of the original TEE sets sur-

vived. Later the TEE label was applied only to the fastest trains on certain routes which were first class only and charged a supplementary fare. TEEs were then both international and national.

In the 1980s the last TEE services were withdrawn. They were replaced by fast two-class services but with varying standards of accommodation. The International Union of Railways decided on a uniform specification for all international services and in 1987 the brand name Eurocity (contracted to EC) was applied to 86 pairs of international trains in Europe.

THE FLYING SCOTSMAN

Flying Scotsman is one of the traditional names on the railways of Britain. When the

former Great Northern Railway introduced a new fast train at 10 a.m. from Kings Cross to Edinburgh in 1862 it was shown in the staff timetables as Special Scotch Express but the public soon dubbed it the Flying Scotsman adapting the legendary name of the Flying Dutchman which had been made familiar in an opera. The name invented by the public has lasted ever since although it was not officially recognized until the Great Northern had been absorbed into the London and North Eastern Railway in 1923. Another tradition was the departure from Kings Cross at 10 a.m. which was maintained almost without interruption until 1982.

Acceleration of trains on all lines soon outstripped the Flying Scotsman in speed. This East Coast Route train was tied by an agreement made with the West Coast Route after the railway "Race to Edinburgh" was brought to an end by the derailment of a West Coast Route express while taking a curve at Preston at high speed. Both parties then agreed that the London–Edinburgh time of daylight trains should not be less than $8\frac{1}{4}$ hours.

With acceleration barred, the London and North Eastern Railway tried other methods of making the Flying Scotsman distinctive. A hairdressing salon and a ladies' retiring room were among new amenities introduced. For a time the train conveyed a cinema coach, and there were experiments in receiving radio broadcasts, to which passengers listened on headphones.

In May 1928 the Flying Scotsman earned worldwide attention by running daily non-stop between London and Edinburgh (392.9 miles/631 km) which at that time was the longest non-stop run in the world. A corridor connection between the leading coach of the train and the locomotive en-

abled the crews to change over at the half-way point on the journey. With no stops en route and still an $8\frac{1}{4}$-hour schedule the going was leisurely compared with running on other lines. At last, in 1932, the $8\frac{1}{4}$-hour agreement lapsed with mutual consent and the long-overdue acceleration of the Flying Scotsman began. By the outbreak of the Second World War the time had been reduced to 7 hours 20 minutes. This was outstripped by the 6-hour schedule of the Coronation streamlined express but the Scotsman was a much heavier train and except in the summer months made stops on the way.

In the 1960s steam locomotives gave place to diesels at the head of the Flying Scotsman and further acceleration took place. HSTs first went into regular service on the Western Region main line between London, Bristol and South Wales in 1976. These were "7+2" formations (seven coaches and two power cars). An extra coach was required on the Eastern Region trains to provide more seating and refreshment service. The first of these longer sets came into operation on the Eastern Region on 8 May 1978. The Flying Scotsman was the fastest train in the new London–Edinburgh service with HSTs. A year later the time to Edinburgh was 4 hours 37 minutes with one stop, at Newcastle.

INTERCITY 125

The British Railways timetable distinguishes services worked by InterCity 125 sets with the letters "IC" at the top of the column.

The driver and his assistant have upholstered seats with armrests. On the driver's side the power controller is a short handle which is moved to and fro to control the engine in his own car and the others in the power car at the rear of the train. When both are running at their top speed of 1,500 rpm they provide 4,500 hp (3,335.6 kW). A knob on top of the handle fits comfortably into the palm of the driver's hand. It is entirely different from the earlier breed of power controllers which seemed often to retain something of the steam locomotive regulator. Indicator lights which normally show blue warn the driver of faults such as overheating or a stopped engine in the rear power car.

The brake controller is similar to the power controller and is on the driver's left. Another small lever by his right hand operates the horn. When it is moved to and fro the horn sounds at full volume for long-range warning in open country. In the other direction the volume is reduced to minimize noise in built-up areas.

This is not a good day for the 09.05 service from London Paddington to Swansea in Wales. An "incident" earlier in the day

Opposite: A poster for the Inlandsbanan, the train which runs for hundreds of miles through the harshest inland zones of Sweden.
Below: Sections of the special rented train of the SJ (Swedish Railways), used by companies and associations for travelling conferences.

has delayed departures of all main-line trains from Paddington. At 09.05 the 09.00 to Weston-super-Mare has not yet left and we know that we shall be on its heels as far as the junction beyond Swindon where the lines to Bristol and to South Wales separate. We are speculating on this situation when a bell rings in the cab – the guard's signal that the train is ready to depart.

A gentle movement of the power handle sets us rolling out of the station, so smoothly that the actual moment of starting has been imperceptible. The power handle has five positions, or "notches," and we are in Notch 2 to limit our speed to the 25 mph (40 kmh) restriction until clear of the station approaches. We are running on the relief line and soon sight a yellow signal ahead warning us to be ready to stop. As we draw close to the signal a siren sounds in the cab, and the driver acknowledges the warning by pressing a button on his desk. If he did not do so the brakes would be applied automatically. At a green

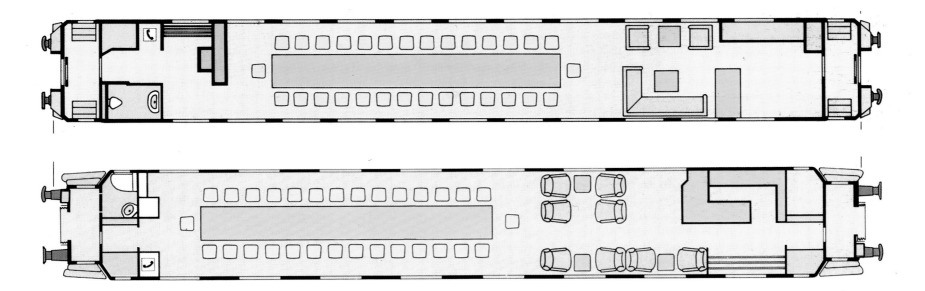

(line clear) signal a bell sounds, and once we are underway we shall hear the bell (hopefully) at short intervals. This time, however, the next signal shows red and we pull up with a hiss of air as the brakes go on. The signal clears and we move over on to the fast line, but not for long. We continue to weave between the fast and relief lines, always under warning signals, as far as Southall, 7½ miles (12 km) from Paddington.

Now at last the driver can pull his controller back and we begin to accelerate, the speedometer creeping up to 125 mph (200 kmh) after a further 10 miles (16 km). With easy going through Maidenhead, where we cross the Thames on Brunel's famous single-span bridge, the power handle is brought back to Notch 4 and speed is held until the siren bleeps and a double-yellow signal warns us to be prepared to stop. Another bleep and a single-yellow signal leads on to a red which brings us to a standstill in sight of Reading station, our first scheduled stop.

We are 25 minutes behind time at Read-

The plate attached to the front of the locomotive hauling the Mistral, as if in challenge to the wind of that name which blows through the Rhône Valley. The famous express covered more than 620 miles (1,000 km) from Paris to Nice in around ten hours. Today the TGVs save some three hours over the same route and lines will soon be extended to Ventimiglia, on the French–Italian frontier, thus serving Monaco and Menton.

ing and on restarting the driver goes at once into Notch 5 – full power. Acceleration is controlled automatically.

After 3 miles (4.8 km) our speed has reached 95 mph (153 kmh) up a slight rise, and reaches 125 mph (200 kmh) on the level which follows. Soon we slow for another yellow, probably warning that we are catching up the train ahead (the belated 09.00 a.m. service to Weston-super-Mare) but a welcome green and a ping on the bell allow us to regain speed. Power is cut off to allow the train to coast for four miles, keeping speed down until we have passed Swindon station. Then it is full power again as we race for Wootton Bassett junction where we shall leave the line to Bristol. The junction is preceded by a yellow signal which flashes to show that the way through the junction is clear at least as far as the first signal beyond it. Further coasting drops our speed to 70 mph (112.6 kmh) and we ride smoothly over the junction points at that speed, the turnout being very gradual so that high-speed trains need not slow unduly.

With power restored after the junction we are running at 110 mph (177 kmh) two minutes later and have just got back to 125 mph when the siren bleeps and we slow down past a yellow signal to stop at a red beyond. Silence descends, apart from the throbbing of the engine behind the almost soundproof door of the engine room. The silence is protracted and the driver climbs down on to the track to telephone to the signalbox. He returns with the resigned air of one who feels that the cards are stacked against him, for the signalman has admitted that he had forgotten our presence. Such a story would be seized upon with delight by the media but we are in the tranquil depths of the English countryside and it will go no further. When we restart we are conscious that we may be unblocking a column of other trains that have been patiently waiting behind us.

The signal has changed to green with what seems to be embarrassed haste and we are on our way against a rising gradient of 1 in 300. We accelerate to 110 mph (177 kmh) before shutting off power to coast through

The golden age of the grand hotels on the Côte d'Azur began at the end of the nineteenth century, thanks directly to the international Genoa–Marseilles railway line and legendary trains like the Mistral and Le Train Bleu. The latter is commemorated by the luxurious restaurant at the Gare de Lyon, Paris, from where trains still depart for the South of France.

Somerton Tunnel. The bore is narrow and if entered at a higher speed the sudden change in air pressure might cause discomfort to passengers.

Power is restored as we emerge from the tunnel and our speed is unchanged as we enter Sodbury Tunnel at the top of a gradient. This is the second longest tunnel on the former Great Western Railway. We stop on the outskirts of Bristol. Company cars abound in the car park, waiting for visitors to local factories or awaiting the return of their owners who have travelled by train to London for a meeting or conference.

There will be no more high speed until after Newport. Coasting at 90 mph (145 kmh) down a gradient of 1 in 100 we enter the eastern portal of the Severn Tunnel, the longest in Britain at 4 miles 683 yds (7 km). The tunnel takes us under the River Severn and soon we see ahead the white marker lights indicating a level section of track where the line is at its lowest point under the river. Power is restored to take us up the gradient which follows and we come

into daylight. This is the limit for most of the remaining few miles to Newport but there is a restriction to 75 mph (120.7 kmh) through the suburbs. After that we cross the River Usk on a viaduct and pull up at the platform in Newport station. It has been far from a copybook journey but gallant efforts have been made to regain most of the arrears of 25 minutes we had suffered by Reading.

LAPPLANDSPILEN

Narvik is the most northerly terminus of the Scandinavian railway system. The warm Atlantic current keeps the port frost-free throughout the year, which made it especially valuable in the strategic planning of the Germans during the Second World War. They captured it in a lightning attack on 9 April 1940 and it marked a critical turning point in the initial phase of the conflict.

Narvik, though part of Norway, is not linked to its rail network, but is in fact the terminus of the Swedish system. Three of Sweden's most famous trains leave from this station: the Bettenviken or Gulf of Bothnia, bound for Göteborg; the Nord-pilen or Arrow of the North, for Stockholm; and the Lapplandspilen, for Malmö. We shall follow the journey of the Lapplandspilen which lasts a little more than 25 hours for a distance of just under 1,250 miles (2,000 km).

The train starts from Lapland, which extends across the northern regions of the three principal countries of Scandinavia and of Russia to the Kola peninsula. This is the far north of Europe, a wild and beautiful land situated between the belt of birches and the tundra. The Lapps live by fishing and by rearing reindeer; during the short

Above: The open spiral track at Brusio, just after the Italian border at Campocologno, on the Bernina line which links Tirano to St Moritz.
Below: The impressive altimetric chart of the Glacier Express which, on its run from St Moritz to Zermatt in Switzerland, crosses three alpine passes (the Albula, the Oberalp and the Furka).
Opposite: The snow-plough keeps the Glacier Express line open all through the year, even above 6,500 ft (2,000 m).
Far right: The carriage indicator card of the famous Swiss train, destined for another popular resort, Davos.

summer they follow the herds to the snow-clad mountains, through areas inhabited by elks, eagles, beavers, lynxes, wolves and bears.

The stations that are dotted along the line leading to the central zones of Sweden, through Dalecarlia, with its gentle hills covered by forests, serve the nearby coal-mines, and as dusk falls their lights glitter brightly and eerily in the gloom, especially at Kiruna, situated below the mine of Luossavaara.

This vast land mass of forests and lakes, with its dark shadows and gleaming reflections, was seen four centuries B.C. by the first great traveller and explorer in history – a Greek from Massilia (Marseilles) named Pytheas – who sailed as far as the island of Thule, then believed to be the most northerly point on earth. Sweden was later to dedicate to his memory a town (Pitea) on the Gulf of Bothnia, between Lulea and Umea. Pitea itself is a stop on one of the sections of line still in service, though infrequently used, of the Inlandsbahn, the old mining railway which runs from Galli-väre to Kristinehamn.

The Lapplandspilen now runs through the famous forests of Dalarna where there are remains of ancient settlements and runes dating from the time of the Celts. Close by are huge lakes – Siljan, Mälar,

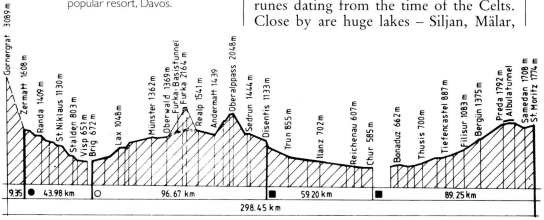

Hjälmar and Vätter – which are evidence of the geological upheavals which affected water levels in the Ice Age.

Early in the morning at Hallesberg the stale and dusty station smells are replaced by the pleasant aroma of leavened dough, cardamom and raisins, ingredients which are used in the traditional Danish pastries. This is Scandinavia's principal rail junction, with lines to Stockholm, Oslo and Göteborg. Apart from its obviously German name, Hallsberg will be remembered in the trivia of railway history for the recent introduction of a very special type of service: the first office on rails – or conference coach as they are now known – in the world (Asea Pendeln). It has 20 fully equipped desks, a conference hall with audiovisual equipment and a lounge. The carriages have telephones linked to the intercontinental network and computers connected to data banks. The prototype, owned by a multinational group, is probably the first private "technical" coach to travel on state railways since the time of

Pullman and Nagelmackers, and it serves the large built-up area between Stockholm and other important business centers such as Eskilstuna, Uppsala and Västeras.

The train now reaches Malmö, facing the Baltic, gateway to Sweden, with its history of victories and humiliations.

It is worth mentioning that until a few years ago another train – significantly called the Meridian – now restricted to the Berlin – Belgrade route, used the Scandinavian rail system. Its original route, as advertised by a few posters still to be found, was wide-ranging: Malmö–East Berlin – Prague – Bratislava – Budapest – Belgrade–Bari. It ended its journey far down the Adriatic at the dilapidated and neglected station of Antivari. This was the last stop on the new line from Belgrade, Yugoslavia's proudly impressive engineering feat which was financed by West German money. It stopped at the foot of the hill where at the beginning of this century Marconi carried out his coast to coast transmission experiments. Sadly, the Meridian was suppressed because of the difficulty in planning a timetable that involved inevitable delays in crossing four problematic frontiers.

MISTRAL

Today this is simply the name of a wind, the strong wind of the Rhône valley, sweeping in from the Swiss Alps and across southern France. It is the wind that ruffled the dresses of the young girls on the bridge at Arles in the paintings of Toulouse-Lautrec and that buffets passengers cruising in the Gulf of Lions. As it gradually loses strength it lashes the western shores of Corsica.

However, Le Mistral was also for gener-

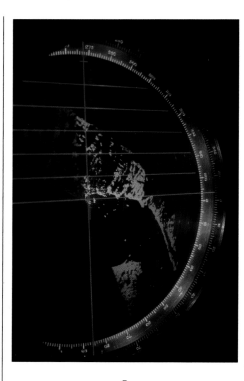

After the Second World War Italian trains were closely linked with the world of work.
Opposite: A passenger greets the driver of a steam locomotive. Soon trains would begin carrying the first Italian emigrants, especially from southern regions, initially to northern Europe (the Belgian coal-mines and the factories of Germany and Switzerland being the main destinations) and later to the cities of the so-called "industrial triangle."
Above: A photogram of the Strait of Messina, used by ferries to carry Sicilian emigrants and also trains routed directly to the cities of northern Italy.

tions the name of the most famous train in France. This was perhaps not as stylish as Le Train Bleu but certainly faster as it sped from Paris to Nice along the Rhône valley almost as if driven by the wind bearing the same name.

It was a journey which epitomized every foreigner's idea of France. The glittering capital with its cabaret shows open until dawn, the early morning wait for the first métro to get to the railway station followed by a breakfast of freshly baked croissants and coffee in the buffet. Bourgeois Lyons, with its austere buildings lined up along the peninsula at the confluence of the river Saône and the Rhône. Then on through the Midi, from Valence to Orange and lovely Avignon with its network of alleys around the Palace of the Popes.

Arriving in Marseilles, Le Mistral reversed into the main station of St Charles near Le Canebière. There you might have seen a couple of officers from the Foreign Legion descending from the train about to embark for Africa, or some shady individuals who looked as though they were embroiled in all manner of mysterious deals. Then past the red rocks of the Estérel into the heat of the Côte d'Azur, with its fashionable beaches, from St Raphael to Cannes and Cap d'Antibes. Finally it arrived at Nice where, beneath the Art Nouveau vaulting of the enormous roof, impoverished gentlewomen mingled with third-rate actresses in search of fame, and dandies headed for the casino.

At the beginning of the 1980s competition pensioned off Le Mistral. In the train's heyday in the early 1970s, most of its business was generated by two very different kinds of passenger: the Lyonnais businessman and the first-class passenger travelling between Paris and the Riviera. The arrival of the TGV (Train à Grand

Vitesse) meant that the 500 miles (800 km) of track from Paris to Marseilles was burned up in 4 hours and 40 minutes.

Le Mistral, although fast, took almost twice that time and cost more. It catered only for first-class passengers, with advance booking (in later years it was known as the TEE [Trans Europ Express]), whereas the TGV also ran a second-class service.

Speed, however, was the principal consideration and this alone was enough to determine the replacement of Le Mistral by the TGV. The French railways have always been proud of their world records for speed. In the 1970s, when the Japanese bullet trains of the Shinkansen line appeared to have robbed them of the title, France responded with the TGV with a view to restoring their supremacy.

GLACIER EXPRESS

The tourists who arrive in Switzerland by car, having negotiated the hairpin bends of the Maloja Pass, do not necessarily take special note of the station of St Moritz. This resort is built on the shores of a small lake which is packed with ice skaters in the winter and yachtsmen in the summer. This is a pity because it is the gateway to the Engadine.

St Moritz is, to some extent, a capital from which the principal alpine lines radiate. Four journeys will bring to life the Belle Epoque to contemporary holiday-makers. The Glacier Express (St Moritz–Zermatt) and Bernina Express (Tirano–Chur) are both long established. The other two are more recent: the Engadine Express, which goes to Vienna, and the Palm Express, which also goes to Zermatt and then across the Alps, via Lugano and

Ascona. These two journeys combine both tourist trains and ordinary trains.

Although all these routes are picturesque, the star attraction of the Swiss railways is undoubtedly the Glacier Express. Scarlet coaches furnished with every comfort are drawn by a shiny locomotive. This legendary train crosses the length of the Alps four times in seven hours, from the valleys of the Inn and the Rhine to the watershed of the Rhône. Clean and efficient there is little concession here to the past except for the old restaurant car, all wood and velvet, and the marvellous twenties-style posters, sold by the bookstalls. The scenery, however, is timeless. Seated before a bowl of steaming fondue, or sipping a cup of chocolate, you can admire the sheer grandeur of the natural surroundings. You find yourself immersed in this magical landscape of firs and waterfalls, and it seems as though you could stretch out and touch the branches outside the window. Then there are the spine-tingling passages across viaducts suspended high over gorges with each curve revealing a new glimpse of crags and peaks.

The line followed by the Glacier Express is a masterpiece of engineering. Even today the boldness of its planning and the way in which it blends so harmoniously with the mountain environment still inspires awe. The section from St Moritz to Disentis includes dozens of bridges, tunnels and spiral curves. Once over the ridge of the Oberalp, which is kept open throughout the year in spite of heavy snowfall, the train reaches the Furka massif. Until a few years ago the train service was interrupted for many months because of the weather conditions; but in 1982 a tunnel more than 7 miles (11 km) long was built to allow trains to run throughout the year. It is the longest narrow-gauge tunnel in the world and the

The frenzied scramble of passengers with their suitcases has long been a familiar sight at major railway stations.

Opposite: An aerial view of the station of Santa Maria Novella, Florence, in the early 1970s. At that time there was heated debate in the Tuscan capital on the subject of an underground railway, which was never realized.

trains also carry cars.

This impressive engineering feat demonstrates the faith of the Swiss in the future of mountain railways. It is by no means a matter of sentimental attachment. These small trains have turned out to be a highly profitable tourist investment. For proof of this just continue your journey beyond Brig to the top of the line at Zermatt. On a clear day, you can lean from the lowered train window and gaze at the unmistakable peak of the Matterhorn in its full splendour. Dozens of cameras will be focused on the sparkling mountain range. The air is crystal clear thanks to the absence of exhaust fumes, since private traffic is banned from the high valley. Alternatively you can take the cogwheel train from Interlaken up to the Jungfrau, thanks to the astonishing system of racks excavated beneath the glacier. There are so many Japanese tourists here that some station signs are in Japanese and the little carriages bear the emblems of twinned Japanese towns.

TRENO DEL SOLE

Italy's domestic rail network is longer than that of any other European country, with the exception of the Scandinavian countries and Russia. The post-war economic boom led to the migration of many workers from the depressed south to the industrial north. In the early 1960s, a staggering 80,000 southern Italians travelled by train to Turin.

The first of the great trains mobilized to handle this large-scale exodus from the 1950s onwards was the Freccia del Sud, (the Southern Arrow), which still operates a daily service between Milan and Sicily. The train thus played a critical role in this

migrational phenomenon. Once Italy's industry was firmly established in the prosperous north, the flow of workers from the poverty-stricken regions of the south was unstoppable. The railways immediately responded to this situation by launching the Triveneto, a highly articulated train with sections from either coast of Sicily which join together at Messina. At Bologna, the train separates again with sections going on to the Brenner, Venice and Trieste.

At the height of the summer season and at Christmas and Easter additional trains were laid on to handle the volume of workers returning to the south for family visits. Anyone beginning a journey from Sicily for the Po valley in the north will be amazed by the astonishing sequence and variety of architectural styles along the way – Arabic, Byzantine, Norman, Catalan, Baroque and Art Nouveau – all in radical contrast to the urban horrors of modern Palermo. As it climbs from the foot of the Italian peninsula, the train seems to pick up speed, rushing through the many long tunnels of the Tyrrhenian coast and past a succession of unmemorable stations. Sleep usually prevents the passengers seeing much of the built-up districts of Naples and Rome, and in any event the Treno del Sole avoids the capital, except for a brief halt in Ostiense station.

CARLO MAGNO AND LEONARDO DA VINCI

In railway history, 30 May 1987 will be remembered for the institution of a high-quality network that involved the whole of western Europe, thanks to the arrival of the Eurocity trains.

These trains have several features in

Above: The writer Robert Musil, an Austrian officer in Italy during the First World War, set one of his splendid stories in the station of Bolzano. *Opposite:* Front view of an E633 locomotive and side view of the Carlo Magno Eurocity train in Milan's Central Station. Connections between Italy and northern Europe depend essentially on the three alpine passes of the Simplon, the Gotthard and the Brenner, which nevertheless cannot possibly cope with the volume of traffic, both passenger and goods, that Europe is likely to see in the twenty-first century.

common: reasonable prices for both first and second class, a fairly high average speed and an efficient and convenient customs inspection, which is carried out before arrival at the frontier. Each of these trains has been given a name with European historical or cultural associations. Milan is the main junction for the two EC (Eurocity) trains that link northern Italy with Dortmund, the northernmost city in the Ruhr basin, connecting the Rhineland and Baltic Germany, by two different routes, except for one common stretch from Mannheim onwards.

Both these trains have existed for years under different names. The first is the Leonardo da Vinci (formerly the Mediolanum), which leaves Milan Central station early in the morning, the other is the Carlo Magno (Karl der Grosse, formerly the Metropolitano) which leaves Dortmund, usually before dawn, and arrives in the evening at Sestri Levante.

Let us take a closer look at the Leonardo. Soon after leaving Milan, the train reaches Lake Garda. The route changes direction in the rocky hills around Verona and begins its climb towards Germany. Now come the first bilingual station signs, which continue as far as the Brenner Pass for 75 miles (120 km). The train stops at the station of Bolzano-Bozen, with its Hapsburg interior. Then it proceeds through the first villages on the Rhine, that evoke the terrible memory of the sealed carriages carrying deportees during 1943–45, their tragic human cargo crowding at the narrow gaps through the cars to catch a last glimpse of the Dolomites. The brief stop at the Brenner, in the station which has become squeezed between the infrastructures of road and rail, evokes memories of the meetings of Hitler and Mussolini which led to the involvement of Italy in the

Second World War.

Beyond the alpine watershed, through the short strip of the Tyrol, the train speeds across Bavaria; the first afternoon stop in Munich furnishes convenient connections to the principal cities in Germany, all of them reached the same day except for Berlin. After aristocratic Augsburg, the impressive Gothic belltower of Ulm appears, dominating the rushing waters of the Danube. Then come verdant Stuttgart, the university town of Heidelberg and the twin cities of Mannheim and Ludwigshafen, nerve centers of the highly efficient German railway system.

One hour later, the Carlo Magno service follows in the Leonardo da Vinci's wake. It stops at Milan and then changes direction for the Gotthard. From Basle the line follows the right bank of the Rhine, the river which for centuries marked the division between the Franks and Saxons, brought

together, or so he imagined, by Charlemagne himself. The train provides spectacular views of the Vosges mountains and the Black Forest, with stops at Freiburg (later, to the left, there is a fleeting glimpse of the suburbs of Strasbourg), Baden Baden and Karlsruhe.

Beyond Mannheim, both expresses follow the left bank of the Rhine, famous in German history and culture, stopping at Worms, Mainz (shortly there will be a distant view of the skyscrapers of Frankfurt and also on the right, beyond the river, of graceful Wiesbaden), the crags of the Lorelei, Coblenz, Bonn, and finally Cologne with its famous twin cathedral spires, which remained intact amid the ruins of the devastated city following the Allied bomling in 1945. Here we enter the major industrial zone, a conurbation which contains centers that symbolize European productivity, such as Wuppertal, Solingen and Leverkusen, and large cities like Dusseldorf, Duisburg, Essen, Bochum and Dortmund, northern apex of the Rhineland–Westphalia–Ruhr triangle.

Dortmund is the terminus for most of the German intercity trains, further examples of the precision and efficiency of the Deutsche Bundesbahn, as well as longer-distance trains such as the Donau Kurier to Prague.

ANDALUS EXPRESO

Thousands of lights from restaurants and night-clubs glitter in the capital which once vied with Belgrade for the dubious honour of being the greyest and dullest in Europe. But "movida," the wish to live, to enjoy oneself, to be modern, has since spread through the whole of Spain, and in Madrid it has now exploded in all its glory. Nor

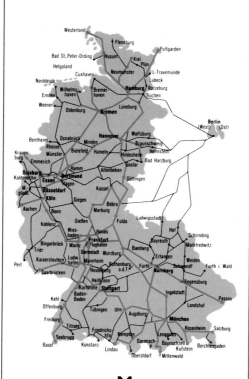

Map of the West German railway network. The DB provides the widest range of intercity services in Europe, shuttling, almost always at regular intervals, between the major German cities, where the "Hauptbahnhof" (main station) is invariably situated in a central position.

have the country's trains escaped this breath of new life.

Until a few years ago the Iberian rail system, cut off from the rest of Europe because of its much wider than normal gauge, seemed consigned to oblivion. The ancient coffee-pot vehicles that wheezed across the highlands of Castile might have been dredged up for some period film; in the south, it would sometimes halt at a *tienda*, the drinking kiosk adjoining a station. "Ten minutes' stop" bellowed the guard, and all the passengers would climb down to seek out a cool spot in the oppressive afternoon heat. Nowadays things have changed and air-conditioned electric trains, whose contours have likewise adapted to modern times, speed along the tracks.

Felipe Gonzales, the Prime Minister, has great plans for his native Andalusia. A new line will greatly shorten the present route and in 1992 it will be possible to travel from Madrid to Seville in only three hours. In 1492 Christopher Columbus made a brief stop in Seville and the city will be celebrating the 500th anniversary of the discovery of America as well as opening a new station, Santa Justa. This will replace the dusty San Bernardo station and also the lovely Plaza de Armas station with its wonderful Arab-style architecture.

Furthermore, with the decision to adjust to the European standard gauge, Portugal will have a third line from the French border to Lisbon. This is part of an attempt to integrate her with other EEC partners in creating a united Europe.

Although there is a wish to retain something of Spain's essential exotic charm, the need has been recognized to throw off the sleepy air, typical of great civilizations fallen into decline. The Spanish railways, with a good sense of timing, have grasped the chance by launching a special train.

It is called the Andalus Expreso. The train does not offer ordinary passenger service so much as a veritable rail cruise that lasts a week. This is a particularly happy formula which already has the advantage of a predecessor in the Transcantabrico, which runs on the narrow-gauge northern line between León, Oviedo and Galizia. That train provides an extremely interesting journey along the wild, windy shores of the Gulf of Gascony, far removed, however, and not just geographically, from what is usually understood by the term *hispanidad*.

The Andalus Expreso combines the impeccable comfort (and prices) of a five-star hotel – single and double sleeping cars, *à la carte* restaurant – with the charm of a land rich in art and cultural treasures, from the Giralda of Seville to the flowered patios of Cordoba. Seven days of roaming by rail

The name Andalus Espreso, here superimposed on to a fan, evokes the gypsy atmosphere of southern Spain.

through the far south with overnight halts in stations so that if you wish to, you can enjoy the flamenco in a local night spot until the early hours. During the day the train visits various places of interest. This makes it one of the most delightful introductions to Andalusia.

Yet all the velvet, fine wood and slightly tinted window glass cannot remove the pathos of a land which retains a deeply dramatic feeling for life, as was evoked so brilliantly in the poems of Garcia Lorca. At Granada you can still alight at the station where, one day in July 1936, the poet ended his last journey. He had fled from Madrid over which the long shadows of the impending civil war were falling. An unhappy choice: Lorca could not have foreseen that assassins in his own city were waiting to kill him.

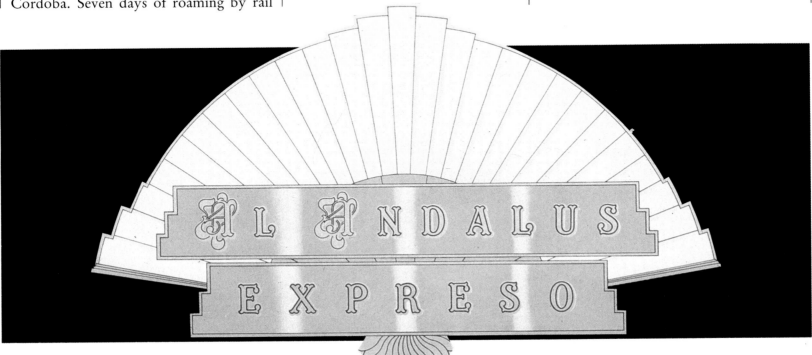

Right: The interior of a tour train immediately conveys an idea of the quality of service to be expected. The concept of holidays by train is now being revived in many countries.

CHOPIN

It was not by chance that the name Chopin was given to the express that leaves Vienna's Südbahnhof every evening at 18.40, crossing the whole of central Poland. This is the land of the great romantic composer and pianist. Marriages between the names of trains and the glories of music have been frequent, if not always pertinent. Austria chose the name of the famous conductor Karl Böhm for a Salzburg–Graz express and Britain named a London–Amsterdam cross-Channel train after the twentieth-century composer Benjamin Britten.

The Chopin was the first train during the years following the Second World War to cross the most difficult frontiers in Europe; not only the so-called Iron Curtain, 32 miles (50 km) north of Vienna, but also the borders between Czechoslovakia and Poland, and between Poland and the USSR.

The Chopin provides direct communication from Vienna to Warsaw by way of the Czechoslovak corridor which, after the constitution of this state, marked the watershed between the country's main regions, Bohemia–Moravia and Slovakia. On its journey the train passes the sinister fortress of the Spielberg, the famous hill of Austerlitz and the shameful extermination camp of Auschwitz, now renamed Oswiecim. Among other derelict places along the route is Teschen, the province disputed between Poland and Czechoslovakia, at the foothills of the Tatra, whose snow-clad peaks rear up dramatically before the monotony of the Sarmatian plain. It is still about 2,500 miles (4,000 km) – equivalent to the distance across the Atlantic from Europe to the United States – before we reach the mighty Urals and the crest of Sverdlovsk, gateway to Siberia.

In the middle of the night the train crosses the gentle Polish plain, for centuries the scene of bitter fighting and servitude. The lights from the hill of Jasna Gora, renowned for the Black Virgin of Czestochova, shine out and the train stops longer than usual to take on a crowd of pilgrims. This is the land of distinguished statesmen, who have included Ben Gurion, Pilsudski, Poniatowski and Ignaz Paderewski, the true founder of modern Poland, and a notable pianist who was an outstanding interpreter of Chopin.

The first light sees the train running through the southern suburbs of Warsaw.

Crossing the Vistula river the train which anticipated the thaw in the Cold War enters the rail corridor linking Moscow and northern Europe. From here the Soviet Union's green carriages depart for Oslo, Stockholm, Malmö, Copenhagen, Brussels, the Hook of Holland, Paris and Berne. From Terespol to Brest Litovsk – which has become the access door to the USSR since the partition of 1939 – a new timetable comes into force (two hours' difference). Both the gauge and customs stops increase. It was here that in December 1917 the Germans, temporarily triumphant, imposed a hard treaty on Trotsky, which was partially thwarted the following November by the Allied victory.

It was here, too, that at 5.25 a.m. on Sunday 22 June 1941, a peaceful train loaded with cereals crossed the frontier from east to west. Poland had not existed as a national entity for almost two years, and the world, in its innocence, was unaware that 3,000,000 soldiers, travelling in 19,000 trains, were at that very moment moving from the Baltic to the Black Sea. Five minutes later German armies invaded Russia and began the gigantic battle between Germany and the Soviet Union which was to continue for four terrible years.

The train nowadays travels at a fast but steady speed; it passes Minsk and Smolensk, the Bug and the Dnieper, heading for the capital. The train thunders over the Beresina river, the site of one of the most horrible episodes in the retreat of Napoleon's army from Moscow and then over the Moscova, a little way from Borodino.

Vast forests and a peripheral ring of roads and railways are signs that the train is approaching Moscow. It was here in mid October 1941 that Guderian's swift armoured columns became bogged down in their vain attempt to break through to Red Square. The locomotive with the red star comes to a halt against the buffers of the Byelorusski, while not far away, another famous Russian train is leaving the Kievski: this is the Pushkin, bound for Athens and Istanbul.

Europe's railways have once again rescued the Orient Express, although restricted nowadays to the Paris–Bucharest run, and no longer enjoying the prestige and glamour of an age that has vanished forever. Today it is the railways of Russia which are reviving the Balkan myth, ever an inherent part of Slav history. The Soviet Union has always been fascinated by Istanbul – more so than Athens – with its many facets and intriguing history. Perhaps it is because the ships of her Black Sea fleet have always been compelled to pass through the Bosphorus. The Occident Express would be an appropriate name.

Opposite:
Czechoslovakian rail tickets.
Below: Warsaw's Starego Miasta, the square rebuilt according to the original plans after the Second World War.

ROSSIA

In the West it is known as the Trans-Siberian, but its proper name is Rossia. This very fact says much about the desire to unify the Slav races which has permeated the conquest – first by the Tsars and then by the USSR – of the territories of the Far East. The Trans-Siberian railway is the longest in the world – 5,773 miles (9,297 km) from Moscow to Vladivostok, 4,884 miles (7,865 km) to Peking across the "short cut" of Mongolia – and, in fact, the Rossia – together with the many other trains that run beside the banks of the Moscova into central Asia and Siberia – is the only true trans-continental express. Today with the demise of the ocean liners this function has been taken over by jet airliners. Nor do the days of the express appear to be numbered, given that short- and long-distance rail traffic is particularly encouraged in the USSR

The construction of the Siberian railways has been a mammoth undertaking, with bridges and tunnels built at temperatures of as low as −50°C for trains which have to keep running to schedule at the same low temperatures. These are slow, comfortable trains; tea is drunk from large steaming cups, guitars are played, and the on-board radio, with its single channel, churns out news bulletins, punctuated with classical music and popular songs of the sixties.

The Russians are very fond of these trains and they are obviously an important part of daily life. The Rossia is always packed when it leaves Moscow's Yaroslavski every afternoon at 14.05 for its six-day journey to the Pacific. It is followed by three more daily trains taking more or less the same route, while four leave the Kazanski for Tashkent. A further two trains leave

In the egalitarian society of the Soviet Union women were employed on the railways long before this happened in other European countries. *Opposite:* The poster for the twinning of the Simplon–Orient Express and the Taurus Express: the only two trains needed in order to travel from Paris to the capitals of the Middle East and to Cairo. The latter journey is no longer possible since the creation of the state of Israel and the troubles in Lebanon.

daily for Alma Ata, over 2,500 miles (4,000 km) from the capital. Twice a week an extra carriage is attached to the Rossia which is bound for North Korea via Ussuriysk, avoiding Chinese territory. This journey holds the record for the longest distance: 6,335 miles (10,200 km) in almost eight days, non-stop.

These are astonishing figures, compared with the train journeys of Europe, but there is an increasing number of tourists who are keen to experience the adventure of the Trans-Siberian Express.

An air of mystery has always surrounded Siberia, partly from the beauty of the taiga – the boundless fir forests which for days are the only sight from the windows as the train proceeds eastward – or perhaps it is the very special atmosphere of the wagon-lit. A huge stove at the end of the carriage keeps the cold out and you get to know the maid who accompanies you right through to your destination. By this time the compartment has become your second home. During the sixties diplomats and journalists took this route in an attempt to interpret developments in the Communist world. Nowadays the journey is undertaken by people in search of adventure or who are curious about life in the East.

It is possible to continue to Japan with a two-day voyage by ship from Nakhodka.

TAURUS EXPRESS

Motor coaches for Anatolia leave the Topkapi bus station in Istanbul, cross the bridge over the Bosphorus and join the colourful and noisy traffic on the roads of Asia. It is possible to reach Mecca without changing.

But if you go by train, your journey will begin in Galata, a busy commercial area of Istanbul. Departing from the jetty a crowded steamer will take you from the Balkan peninsula to Asia Minor in just a few minutes. It drops you at the station of Haydarpaşa with its architectural style reflecting its Germanic origins. The Turkish rail network – the company initials are TCDD – has not been as fortunate as the private motor car. Although planned years ago, the railway bridge or tunnel across the Bosphorus has still not appeared. The Thomas Cook timetable indicates a four-hour wait at the station of Sirkeci for any passenger arriving from Europe who wants a connection for Asia.

In the opposite direction there is at least an eight-hour wait and this fact, reflecting foreseeable train delays, helps to explain the sharp contrast that always appears as the rail traveller proceeds from north to south. Haydarpaşa, "port of the South," is a microcosm of the races, languages, religious faiths, political interests, enmities and mysteries that make up the Middle East.

The Taurus Express departs from here on its 1,580-mile (2,543-km) journey to Aleppo and Baghdad. Its name comes from the Taurus mountain range which separates the Anatolian highlands from the Mediterranean coast. Until 1976, with a change in Syria, it was possible to reach Beirut in just over two days. Probably little now remains of the station of the St

George's quarter among the ruins of what used to be one of the most glittering capitals of the Levant. Though recently, after some ten years, a suburban train returned timidly to run as far as the Jbeil citadel (ancient Biblos).

In the 1970s the "road to the Indies" began at Istanbul. Innumerable young people went in search of spiritual or artificial paradises on the beaches of Goa or in the valleys of Katmandu. They could take a direct connection to Teheran and then continue by bus to Afghanistan, still enveloped in its feudal atmosphere. With the seizure of power by the ayatollahs in Iran, the service has been "temporarily suspended." The TCDD trains do not go further than Kapikoy, the last Turkish outpost 1,250 miles (2,000 km) east of Istanbul. The journey involves a ferry trip across the enormous Lake Van to the foot of Mount Ararat.

The only international connection – somewhat dangerous – is between Syria and Iraq. Diplomats in the Middle East, in any event, no longer need the train for their comings and goings: no government official or businessman would dream of spending three days to cover the distance from the Golden Horn to the valley of the Euphrates.

The railway built by the Kaiser to seal his alliance with the crumbling Ottoman Empire is today used by emigrants attracted by the dream of finding work in Vienna or Düsseldorf, by veiled women who belie the Turkish claim to have established the first secular Muslim country, and high-ranking army officers of NATO posted to barracks on the eastern frontier.

And then there are the detainees on leave, as depicted in *Yol*, the "on the road" film masterpiece by the unfortunate Ylmaz Güney. Turkish is a difficult language but in some respects it follows European idioms. Like the German *bahn*, the word *yol*, "street," has also come to mean "railway."

HIMALAYAN QUEEN

The station is simply called "Junction," like hundreds of others scattered all over the former British Empire. The term is closely associated with the railways, like the Spanish *empalme* or the Portuguese *entroncamento*, evoking the image of a remote spot in the countryside built by the authorities at the meeting point of lines carrying traffic of varying importance. In this instance the Junction is in the center of the capital of one of the most heavily populated countries in the world, a short distance from the Red Fort and the colourful and crowded market of Chandni Chowk.

The station of Old Delhi, like thousands of other stations in the Indian subcontinent, is as fascinating today as it was in the early twentieth century. Bearded men in turbans, rag-clad young women with radiant smiles, sellers of spice and tobacco, beggars, children and animals of all kinds mill about in colourful activity.

The sultry heat envelops both sumptuous palaces and sordid shanty towns, and you cannot see the mountains though the Himalayas are not that far away. The greatest mountain range on Earth dominates the Ganges valley and protects, to the north, the "imperial way." This was first a river, then a caravan route, and finally a railway. Over the centuries it has seen a succession of conquerors and rulers, from the Mogul emperors to the viceroys of the British Empire.

The Himalayan Queen leaves each morning from Kalha and takes only a few

Evocative pictures of the railway in India.
Opposite: The Toy Train, which climbs from Siliguri to Darjeeling in about seven hours. The service, on a line with normal traction but narrow gauge (the width between the two rails is only 760 mm) has recently been suspended and may be closed forever.

hours to reach the Himalayas. When the slopes get steeper, you have to change trains.

The railroad, very wide according to today's standard gauge (1.676 mm), is reduced to less than half (0.762 mm) to allow the more flexible and smaller trains to climb as far as Simla, negotiating extremely sharp curves and breathtakingly deep gorges.

Often people say that the Indian railways are dangerous. From time to time there is a news item in the local paper about a bandit attack on a train in Rajistan. It is also hard to forget the disastrous accident in 1981 which cost the lives of a thousand people. A cow strayed on to a bridge, derailing a train which plunged into the raging river below. Apart from such catastrophic events – Asian tragedies always seem to be on a more massive scale than elsewhere – incidents of pickpocketing, theft and gratuitous violence are certainly more frequent at Penn station, New York, than at Egmore station in Madras.

The exterior appearance of the coaches is unlikely to encourage the Western traveller. The tiny windows are protected by a grille and a crowd of illegal passengers crouch on the roof in defiance of the inspectors. What is less immediately obvious is the brutal relationship between man and machine. It is still extremely hard work to be an engine driver in India, especially when you have to shovel coal into the furnace of one of the steam locomotives still in service, and that at 45°C in the shade. Nobody knows the exact temperature of the heated metal plates in the driver's cabin.

The passenger should also take precautions. The travel guide advises the tourist to close the badly fitting window to avoid dust from the plain and specks of soot from invading the compartment. After a night's travelling, it may still be necessary to shovel up the ash that has collected on the floor.

The mountain trains are more bearable because you can crouch on the steps and enjoy the fresh breeze blowing from the heights. If Simla is the closest "alpine" destination to Delhi, the wealthy citizens of Bombay are regular devotees of the Math-

eran Hill Railway. The most spectacular of all the "toy trains" which scale the mountains is that of Darjeeling.

It takes eight hours to cover the 54 miles (87 km) that separate the Brahmaputra valley from this ledge in the clouds and is well worth the effort. Darjeeling seems like a different world. The terraces of tea plantations have gradually replaced the forests. Children run after the puffing train and

often appear in front of it on the curves.

It was the British who built this incredible line, in the land of the legendary Gurkhas, to enable the families of their officials to get away occasionally from the miseries and oppressive heat of Calcutta.

NORTH STAR

On one side, towards the yellowish river, are the pagodas which surround the Royal Palace, with the throng of tourists assembled under the tropical sun. Beyond here, when darkness falls, Europeans, Americans and Japanese seek the more dubious pleasures offered by the crowded discos around the embassies. Standing amongst all this is the austere railway station of Krungthep. The iron ceilings bring to mind some of the Paris stations.

There are not many foreigners waiting for the trains that leave from Bangkok. The reason is simple. Some 125 miles (200 km) to the east is the Kampuchean border near Aranyaprathet, with its camps of refugees waiting to return to their unhappy country. Nobody even talks of going farther. The train reaches Nong Khai in the north – but after that comes the Mekong and the inscrutable land of Laos – or Chiang Mai, the ancient capital, where the mountains swarm with guerrillas and opium merchants.

At most you can take a trip to Kanchanburi, site of the bridge over the River Kwai. This was where the "railway of death" crossed the river. The Japanese forced prisoners-of-war to build it in order to supply their troops stationed in Burma and Assam.

There is a special train for tourists and relatives who come to pay respects at the Allied cemetery. It leaves early, at 6.35 a.m.

Above and below: The original name plates of two famous hotels in Indochina. The distance by train between the two cities is about 1,250 miles (2,000 km), along the narrow Malacca peninsula. *Opposite:* A young engine driver from South Vietnam in the cab of a brand-new locomotive built with money provided by the US government. The emblem of the two grasped hands is intended to symbolize the beginning of the period of cooperation between the two nations.

Otherwise there is a southbound train from Bangkok. It is no mean undertaking; a journey of almost 1,250 miles (2,000 km) along the narrow Malaccan peninsula and two days' travel to Singapore. The heat is only made supportable by the providential air-conditioning in the wagons-lits. The train has the near-unpronounceable name of Ekspres Antarabangsa, but many know it as the North Star. It used to carry British officials and wealthy Chinese merchants to wonderful sounding destinations in Southeast Asia.

Thailand is a long, narrow country. Although in the atlas Bangkok appears to be situated in southern Thailand, an entire afternoon and night have passed since leaving the capital and still there is no sight of the Malaysian customs. It is 10 a.m. before passengers have to alight at Padang Besar.

At Butterworth they change trains. This is not really necessary since the gauge on both sides of the frontier is the same. They can take advantage of the stop to interrupt their journey and visit nearby Penang, situated on an island recently linked to the mainland by an impressive road viaduct. For those who prefer not to use modern transport, there is always the old funicular which offers a splendid aerial view of the city.

It is still 243 miles (391 km) to Kuala Lumpur, with its monumentally grand station, and the same again to Johore Bahru, the last Malaysian town since Singapore chose the path of independence. The train crosses the wide bridge joining the mainland to the small island-state, dissected by countless roads. Within a few minutes the Third World has been left behind and the passengers disembark into one of the most sophisticated modern cities.

When you come out of the main station,

it is advisable to be careful. If you so much as drop a cigarette stub you risk a heavy fine. And you will look in vain for a sampan or rickshaw driver among the skyscrapers of the equatorial Manhattan called Singapore. Asia, for the time being, seems a world away.

REUNIFICATION TRAIN

The first train left from Saigon, now renamed Ho Chi Minh City, on 31 December 1976. Four days later, with cheering crowds on either side, it reached the Hang Co station in the capital of Hanoi, 1,075 miles (1,730 km) to the north. At last one of the world's most afflicted railway lines was again operating along its entire length.

The French built the line in 1936, as a final consolidation of their rule over Indochina. Since then the narrow strip of land nowadays known as Vietnam – pressed between the mountains and the China Sea – has known very few years of peace. In 1941 the Japanese began by invading Indochina and France was obliged to yield military control. Soon after the end of the Second World War the Vietminh war of independence broke out. For eight years French troops were engaged in the struggle until the battle of Dien bien phu when they were heavily defeated. Already damaged by frequent attempts at sabotage, the railway line was finally cut in two in 1954. An iron bridge over the Bo Dien river was blown up and what remained symbolized the irreparable break-up of the country into two parts – the Communist North and the pro-American South. During the 1960s the Washington government endeavoured somehow to repair the southern part of the line linking Saigon with Danang and the ancient capital of Hue, terminating at

Quang Tri, just south of the ceasefire line.

The new diesel locomotives which arrived from General Motors bore the emblem of cooperation, two hands grasping each other above the American flag. Even specimens of the "Wickham trolley" – a sort of armoured car on rails formerly used by the British to put down the Communist rising in Malaysia – were recycled. This time they proved useless in overcoming the stubborn resistance of the Vietcong.

Bit by bit the line was blown up and the repair teams were repeatedly attacked by new saboteurs. The American bombers helped to complete the work of systematic destruction. In the North, Ho Chi Minh's government, in an attempt to save what remained of the infrastructure, dismantled bridges and railways and took them to caves in the mountains. In Hanoi the old trams built by the French continued to run with hooded headlights.

When Saigon was captured by the Vietcong, the modest main-line station buildings were still intact in the town center, and orders were given for reconstruction. But in the spring of 1975 very little remained of the line. Many trunk lines had been converted into roads or paths, others had been blocked by unauthorized buildings or even by military airports. The rest were overgrown with grass and weeds which, when they came to be cleared, were found to conceal a variety of deadly snares: unexploded bombs, booby traps and electric circuits. Yet in little less than 12 months the train was able once again to run from north to south, helping to heal the wounds of so many years of war and separation. For this reason it was named the Reunification Train, leaving every evening from Hanoi at 21.20 and from Ho Chi Minh City at 20.23. Almost three days

are still needed to complete the entire journey.

The train from Peking, which during the long war against the Americans had sent military advisers and diplomatic observers, no longer runs to Hanoi. Once again the railways have had to pay for the whims and caprices of history.

CANADIAN

Only in 1871, when the states of Manitoba, Saskatchewan and Alberta came to recognize the enormous farming and commercial potential of their central plains regions, did work begin on the building of a railway line across the whole of Canada. It took 15 years to complete, because of the many practical difficulties encountered. The line ran through territories swept by arctic blizzards and crossed the Rocky Mountains. This range, which virtually protects the west coast, continues down into lower California and then re-emerges, as the Andes, stretching in the southern hemisphere as far as Cape Horn. The 2,878 miles (4,663 km) from Montreal to Vancouver could well be described as a "Trans-Siberian of the West," since both the landscape and climatic conditions are very similar. The line also leads, though with various changes of direction, to the Pacific. In a sense, the Canadian line is more truly intercontinental, and certainly longer, than those of the neighbouring United States, which start from Chicago.

This route should ideally be extended to the Atlantic, to the terminal of Halifax in Nova Scotia, through Quebec and the vast St Lawrence estuary, where the great explorer from St Malo, Jacques Cartier, landed in 1534. The journey across Canada leaves the Gare Centrale in the heart of

Opposite: A train of the Canadian Pacific Railway, photographed around 1870, with the characteristic large funnel typical of the earliest American locomotives. Today Canadian Pacific is one of the major national companies which owns, in addition to a transcontinental rail network, trucks, ships and a fleet of aircraft. The passenger trains are managed directly by the government in Ottawa under the name of "Via Rail."

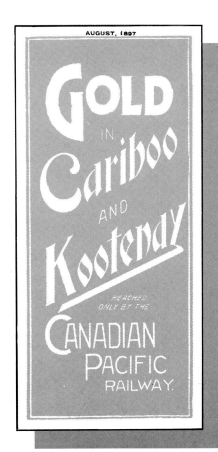

AUGUST, 1897

GOLD IN Cariboo AND Kootenay

REACHED ONLY BY THE

CANADIAN PACIFIC RAILWAY.

Montreal. Until quite recently there were two transcontinental expresses which ran along adjoining routes, one belonging to the colossal private company Canadian Pacific, the other to the state railroad, Canadian National. When the decision was made to do away with the unprofitable sector of passenger traffic, the two trains were combined by the federal agency Via Rail to form a single luxury train, the Canadian. The other name – Supercontinental – was retained for the Winnipeg – Prince Rupert run, perhaps rather a grand title for a journey of some 1,476 miles (2,378 km).

Montreal, a city only about 200 years old, has its modern skyscrapers but also its Latin quarter. The old town resembles the center of Rouen, and the high ground of Mont Royal is somewhat like Montmartre. Its European origins are more obvious than in similar cities over the border in the United States. Montreal is connected to New York by the Adirondack, the express which runs through the Adirondack National Park, the historic region of Saratoga Springs and the Hudson valley, ending up in Manhattan.

The Canadian was extremely comfortable, its panoramic coaches providing some of the most marvellous scenic views to be enjoyed from any train in the world. Moreover, the railway maintenance is far superior in Canada to that in the United States (the former has recently suspended service of the nightly Montrealer because the roadbed north of Springfield does not conform to minimum safety regulations). Maintenance was a critical factor, given that this journey lasted 70 hours, which is not much considering the obstacles encountered. Only in 1916 did the Transcanadian come into its own. Before this, for example, four locomotives were needed to haul a mere ten coaches over the steep gradient of the Kicking Horse Pass.

The train passed the federal capital of Ottawa where the Parliament building on the hill looks from a distance like that of Westminster. It then continued through the state of Ontario past the many lakes and forests (including the celebrated Algonquin Park). With almost a third of its journey done, the train reached Thunder Bay, on the northern shore of stormy Lake Superior.

With Manitoba in view, the train would then set off across the immense prairie. This area produces much of the world's grain and stretches for another third of the total distance as far as the Rocky Mountains.

A picture showing the opening of a new line in Quebec, 6 November 1957. Although Canada has a far smaller population than the United States, it has, unlike its neighbour, not neglected its rail system. The harsh climatic conditions during the long subarctic winter in Canada often make it extremely difficult to travel by air and automobile, accounting for the popularity of the train as a means of transport.

Opposite: A panoramic view of Vancouver, Canada's port on the Pacific, which owed its growth to the arrival of the transcontinental railway line.

From Winnipeg a branch line of 1,000 miles (1,600 km) leads to Hudson's Bay, associated with the discovery of the Northwest Passage, the fur trade and the red-coated Mounted Police.

After Calgary, bristling with oil wells, the train tackled the first foothills of the Rockies and ran through the immense national parks. These parks are evidence of the far-sighted policy of nature conservationists and they provide ideal pastures for elks and bears. Here one can see how the railway is the least environmentally harmful mode of transport. The train wound through a forest which is recovering from the intensive tree-felling programmes of the last century. Like a huge snake through the dense curtain of greenery, the line touched Banff and Lake Louise, where even the outline of the occasional hotel does not greatly disturb the majestic harmony of the region.

The following morning the train would cross the broad valley of the Fraser river.

This was the destination of gold-diggers in the late nineteenth century. Soon it would reach Vancouver, looking much like any other modern city which has recently sprung up with tall buildings. It still retains a somewhat British flavour, rather like Sydney and Cape Town. The city is named after the navigator who accompanied Captain Cook on his voyages across the Pacific. Today it is the third largest city in Canada, despite its rather isolated situation. Although it faces north towards the windswept wastes of Alaska, it has a rainy but mild climate.

This service was much lamented by railway devotees on its closure. Falling passenger numbers, however, made the end of the service inevitable.

PANAMA LIMITED

At the time of Prohibition, gambling was rife all over America, swept by the fever of the "roaring twenties." The paddle steamers of the Mississippi, already superseded as a means of transport by the newly introduced trains, survived more or less as regular gaming houses, with their clientele of playboys and ladies of easy virtue. However, the fascination of the green baize table had already been transferred from the rivers to the railroads.

Often it was the guard who would run the tables, receiving a generous tip or perhaps a percentage of the winnings. Nowhere were the pleasures and dangers of poker pursued with such eagerness as on the train known as the Panama Limited, during its 18-hour journey from the shores of Lake Michigan to the Gulf of Mexico.

The starting point of this run was the busy city of Chicago, teeming with gangsters and millionaires who had grown rich overnight on the production and wholesale commerce in grain and livestock. At the end of the run, almost 939 miles (1,500 km) to the south, lay sleepy New Orleans, still basking in the late colonial torpor of the Vieux Carré, unmistakably French in taste and style. There the steamers were waiting to leave for Panama or Havana and the delights and vices of the Caribbean, Cuban cigars, Creole girls and shady deals among the plantations of the banana republics.

The journey was far from boring, although the flat prairie landscape outside was unremarkable, a complete contrast to the views of the Rocky Mountains to be seen on board the Empire Builder or the Californian Zephyr. But in the comfortable Pullman cars, even for those who did not play cards or gamble, there was always the chance of enjoying a pleasant evening

The streamlined contours of a locomotive during the years when private companies in the United States were still endeavouring to develop passenger traffic.
Opposite: A poster for the Mexican Central, a private railway company, later nationalized, advertising Mexico as "the Egypt of the New World" because of her architectural treasures.

listening to jazz or the blues, played on the piano or saxophone by young musicians from the deep South.

Today things have changed. The train is still there, though running under the federal colours of Amtrak. It is now called City of New Orleans, the name of another famous train from the days of private companies, when there were many daily expresses running between the two cities.

In downtown Chicago, which for a time suffered from the crisis in the heavy industry but is now undergoing a revival, Union station remains as lively as ever, perhaps the busiest station in North America.

The terminal of New Orleans is close to the futuristic Superdome stadium. It looks rather sad, for it is practically deserted, with only the Crescent from New York and Atlanta to supplement the daily train from Chicago. The Sunset Limited for Houston and Los Angeles is scheduled to leave only three times a week. Nothing else pulls up along the rows of abandoned platforms. There have not been any commuting trains for years.

Nor do the steamers for Panama any longer tie up at the wharves of the Mississippi; anyone wishing to get to Central America must go by air, unless sufficiently adventurous to spend days of travel, with numerous frontier stops, on a Tica bus, the Hispanic counterpart of the famous Greyhound.

For Boston and Detroit businessmen, however, the Vieux Carré retains a European charm which fully justifies a trip to Louisiana. Bourbon Street is certainly still the most elegant of America's streets of sin and the old streetcars depicted in Tennessee Williams' famous play still trundle along St Charles Street.

124

AGUILA AZTECA

The Rio Grande marks the border between the United States and Mexico. On one side of the river lies affluent Texas, hardly affected by the recent fall in the price of oil. On the other bank groups of desperate Mexicans wait for darkness in a bid to smuggle themselves across into the land of their dreams. They are driven by the hope of earning money, perhaps as a farmhand in the fast-developing Sun Belt or as a dishwasher in some St Louis restaurant.

Until a few years ago a train from Chicago, bearing the somewhat pompous name of Inter-American, ran to Laredo, Texas. It has now been renamed The Eagle and its route ends farther north at San Antonio. The only way now of reaching Laredo is by taking the Greyhound. Amtrak, the federal agency in charge of railroad services, removed the link with the southern border. In the United States the train has been an expensive and rather upper-class form of transport. They obviously felt it was pointless trying to find customers among the under-privileged Mexicans, and more profitable to exploit links with Toronto and Montreal.

On the other side of the Rio Grande it is a different situation and one can pick up the train again. The Nacional de Mexico, though it lacks the advantages of the bus in terms of speed and frequency of connections, has not relinquished its job of serving passengers, as has happened in many parts of North America. So from the border with the United States you can travel to Mexico City from some seven different departure points, including Mexicali, opposite Calexico in California, arriving eventually at Matamoros, on the Gulf. But the quickest and shortest journey – although it still takes 23 hours to cover the

760 miles (1,226 km) – is on the Aguila Azteca. This train leaves from Nuevo Laredo which is twinned with the adjoining Texan town of Laredo. Thus another eagle ("aguila" means eagle in Spanish) has been chosen as the emblem of a famous train. The Mexicans, however, are proud of their descent from noble pre-Colombian stock and would disclaim any connection with its "Yankee" counterpart.

On its way to the capital the train crosses the desolate, sun-baked northern highlands. It then skirts the industrial zone of Monterrey and descends towards the *meseta*. This is the setting for the exploits of Pancho Villa, hero of the rural revolution who is always portrayed on horseback, although even he was not averse to the more comfortable train to take him to the city of Torréon.

The station of Querétaro may remind some people of the romantic and tragic fate of Maximilian of Habsburg. He was crowned Emperor of Mexico in 1864 under the protective wing of Napoleon III, but he was finally shot, after the French withdrew their support, by the troops of Benito Juárez, the President of Mexico.

A little farther west, beyond the *sierra*, is Guanajuato. This romantic city is also served by a local "mixed" train. In Latin America not many trains offer the comforts of the Aguila Azteca, with its air-conditioning and wagons-lits for single passengers and families. But the brave can avail themselves of a number of these "mixed" trains which combine passenger coaches and goods wagons.

At Buenavista, the terminus of the capital, you are welcomed by the epigram: "Viajar no solo es llegar, tambien es ver y conocer," which, roughly translated, points out that travelling does not merely mean arriving but also seeing and understanding. For the true traveller the journey is more important than the destination.

TREN DE SIERRA

Since the last trams disappeared from Lima in 1965 – a strike of personnel led to the immediate curtailment of the whole service – everyone travels by car or bus. Until a few years back, this unenviable record was shared, among modern cities, by Caracas. However, when the French provided the Venezuelan capital with a technically advanced train system, Lima was left sadly alone with its plans for urban trains yellowing in some ministerial drawer.

Yet there is a railway station in Lima. It is centrally situated, just behind the presidential palace, a couple of steps from the Plaza de Armas. Like all important stations, this neoclassical building is not without a certain elegance. It is called Desemparados. The two lines running along the embankments of the Rimac river carry only a single train in and out, and that only three times a week. This is obviously somewhat inadequate for a city of at least five million inhabitants.

Yet nobody who cares about railways should strike Lima off the list of possible destinations. The orange coaches which stand idly alongside the platform of Desemparados at 7.40 a.m. are not part of any ordinary train, but the Tren de Sierra, which runs along the highest line in the world. It takes five hours to ascend from sea level to the pass just beyond the station of Ticlio, at a height of 15,840 ft (4,829 m).

The entire operation is all the more astonishing because it uses no special mechanical device, neither rack and pinion nor funicular. Using simple traction and standard gauge, the track climbs the moun-

A monument erected in honour of the patron of railways in a small station in Peru.
Opposite: Indians take their ease in the fields at one of the stops the train makes on the Puno–Cuzco line.
Opposite far right: A postcard showing Ticlio, a small Peruvian station famous for being the highest in the world: 15,665 ft (4,800 m) above sea level. The Tren de Sierra, leaving from Lima, on the Pacific coast, reaches Ticlio in just over four hours.

tain ridges in nine sharp zigzags. This means that the train has to reverse direction 18 times. At every bend the locomotive in front has to push while the one in the rear drags the multicoloured coaches backwards.

The higher the train goes, the thinner the air becomes. Any passenger not accustomed to high altitude may experience the symptoms of altitude sickness. The Indians of the Sierra, descended from the legendary Incas, wrapped in their ponchos of coloured wool, stare impassively at the tourist whose face gradually begins to turn purple. When the condition threatens to become dangerous, a nurse with an oxygen bottle rushes up to resuscitate the unfortunate passenger.

In a sense the train represents the belated revenge of the Indians over the colonists. The Ferrocarril Central del Perù was built at the end of the nineteenth century with their sweat and blood, together with that of Chinese immigrants who had crossed the Pacific to escape repeated famines.

Working at high altitude, sometimes teetering on the edge of an abyss, was bad enough, but the sufferings of the labour force were increased by the risk of being bitten by the poisonous insect known as the *verruga*.

A relic of that grim and tragic period remains in the clothing of the people of the Andes. The Indian and *mestizo* women still wear with pride the black bowler hat that their grandmothers saw on the heads of the British engineers who had come to supervise the railway workers.

This railroad was intended to link Lima and Buenos Aires, constituting the backbone of a Latin American communication system. Then history intervened decisively and the Peruvian tract between Huancayo and Cuzco was never constructed. Beyond

Huancayo, terminus of the Tren de Sierra, only a narrow-gauge trunk line leads through terrifying gorges and chasms to distant Huancavelica.

Yet when the only daily train from Lima arrives, the Indians pay it the honour which one would expect to be accorded to a real Pan-American express. On either side of the line they wait in their hundreds in the hope of selling the occasional tourist an alpaca sweater or a *chullos* cap. They await the train patiently for a whole day.

127

LAGOS DEL SUR

The station of Plaza Constitucion, not far from the harbour districts where the tango was born, fits well into the homogeneous urban architecture of Buenos Aires. A metropolitan line runs to Retiro, the largest railway terminus in the capital, where trains from the northern and central parts of the country converge.

Plaza Constitucion, however, is the departure point of lines for the two most famous tourist routes in Argentina, one towards Mar del Plata, the elegant Atlantic resort with its enormous sandy beach, the other to San Carlos de Bariloche.

The line to San Carlos de Bariloche was recently put into service. It negotiates the south-western slopes of the Andes and constitutes the extreme southern limit of the American railway system, except for the isolated mining line of the Rio Gallegos in Patagonia.

Two other trains leave at about the same time in the morning. The Stella Maris covers 250 miles (400 km) in less than five hours, towards the northern beaches. The Lagos del Sur covers 1,085 miles (1,750 km) in 32 hours, travelling across the pampas towards the snow-capped peaks of the Cordigliera.

The train travels almost at road level through the seemingly endless residential districts bisected by wide avenues. It

128

Some of the carriages that make up the Lagos del Sur, including a cinema car, much appreciated for relieving the monotony of long journeys across the pampas.
Opposite: Map of the FA (Ferrocarriles Argentina) network. It is still possible to travel by train from the Paraguayan frontier to Patagonia.
Opposite far right: A poster commemorating the centenary of the Argentine Republic in 1910.

eventually comes out into a broad region of sheltered, cultivated fields, interspersed with neat, pretty villages. The language of the Argentinians who chatter away in the crowded compartment is almost as resonant as pure Catalan, often accompanied by hand gestures. The tables of the restaurant car are particularly lively.

The entire day is spent travelling through unvarying yet pleasant scenery. The passenger can really appreciate a sense of tranquillity from the vast open space beyond the window. The express itself seems content just to make steady headway, seldom venturing beyond 35–45 mph (60–70 kmh). The names of the stations, which become more and more basic like simple shelters for the gauchos, bear the names of flowers and colours: Cañuelas, Las Flores, Azul, Olavarria, until the terminus of Bahia Blanca. From here the line branches off to Zapala. It heads west, like the other main lines of the Argentinian network. This consists of about 18,600 miles (30,000 km) of track, beginning with the Buenos Aires–Mendoza route, plus the 620 miles (1,000 km) that twist up towards Aconcagua.

As night falls, the train plunges into the pampas, the vast grassy plains of Argentina. Despite the inexhaustible wealth of livestock in this the world's biggest pasture it has not led to national prosperity. The country has been in a precarious situation

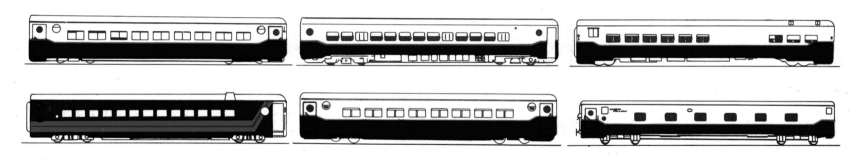

since the nineteenth century and has never managed to achieve economic stability. The hallowed *peso* became practically worthless and with the return to democracy the new *austral* was also soon caught up in the endless spiral of inflation.

During the brief midnight stop at the station of Carmen de Patagones, the train, now facing the direction of the legendary Cape Horn, is buffeted by the cold, dry wind known as the *pampanero*; even blasts of wind from the Pacific sweep away the clouds from the black sky. There is no Milky Way, Plough or the Pleiades, just one huge expanse devoid of any bright landmark, only the solitary beacon of the Southern Cross.

The bogies and the brake system are continuously tested by the slope. Daylight reveals a mountain landscape with very clear air full of the smell of freshly cut timber and the scent of pines. At midday of the second day the train passes through a tiny station called after Jacobacci, the Italian engineer who built this last, almost impassable stretch of railway. At dusk the most famous train of the Argentine railway system ends its climb of the Andes and lets off a small group of passengers. This often includes railway enthusiasts and elderly villagers who are afraid of undertaking the journey by air.

San Carlos de Bariloche – which everyone simply calls Bariloche – is somewhat reminiscent of a Swiss Alpine resort, with big hotels built around a lake. It has always been a favourite holiday spot for rich Argentinians. In the years following the Second World War many individuals associated with the Nazi regime fled here and were warmly received by the Perons.

At night the Tyrolean outline of the slender belltower of the cathedral, which reflects a Late Gothic style, stands out.

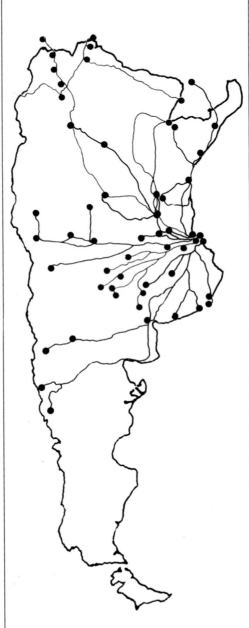

From the balcony of the Hotel Roma one sees the receding street lights and the snowfields beyond. Although reaching this outpost is supremely satisfying, our gaze turns south towards boundless Patagonia, the disputed Falklands, Tierra del Fuego and its capital Ushuaia – the last town in the world – and finally Antarctica.

GHAN

The roads, straight and monotonous, are lined up neatly from east to west within the radius of little more than a kilometer. Situ-

ated at the four points of the compass, they are not called "streets" but "terraces," and they surround the city center of Adelaide. In whatever direction you go, you come to one of the huge parks that lead to the suburbs, urban playgrounds like none to be found in overcrowded Europe or in America, prisoner to the iron laws of real estate profit.

Beyond West Terrace, bordered by the grassy stretches of Park Lands, is Keswick station. It is worth savouring this abundant greenery because, once you have boarded the Ghan, which leaves every Monday and Thursday for Alice Springs, 965 miles (1,555 km) to the north, all you see are rare yellowing bushes in the midst of a flat expanse of desert. The journey lasts 22 hours.

Today, instead of "nothing" there is Alice Springs, with a few thousand inhabitants living in small houses built strictly to a plan. But the town is also a bold testimony to man's powers of adaptation, for it is probably the most isolated civilian populated area in the world. All around, for a thousand kilometers or more, there is nothing but sand, brushwood, stunted bushes and sunbaked rocks. There is also the most celebrated monument of all, Ayers Rock, a major tourist attraction of a region otherwise neglected. It is a monolith almost 2 miles (3 km) long and 1,100 ft (335 m) high, which changes colour several times a day, according to the position of the sun: one of the few marvels of nature which still have the power to astonish the blasé modern traveller.

There is no better way to get there than by the Ghan, in an air-conditioned wagon-lit, with large drinks served in the restaurant car and perhaps with your car – preferably large-wheeled to cope with the rough terrain – also transported by the

The Ghan, one of the two great trains of the Australian desert, covers the 965 miles (1,555 km) of its Adelaide–Alice Springs run in under 24 hours.

Opposite: The famous Australian steam locomotive Puffing Billy, lovingly restored, is frequently used for special commemorative trains and tourist trips.

same train at the rear.

It is unlikely that in road-crazy America or even in Europe that a small town such as Alice Springs would be considered worth furnishing with a short branch railway; but here in the Antipodes, fortunately, things are different.

Only in 1980 was the old narrow-gauge line which ran farther east abandoned when the new standard-gauge line was opened. Once a week the direct train from Sydney, almost 1,860 miles (3,000 km) away, arrives at Alice Springs.

However, the plan is even more ambitious, eventually extending the railway to Darwin, Australia's extreme northern outpost on the Timor Sea. Early in the next century the second Trans-Australian line is expected to come into service, after the first east–west line which terminates in Perth.

There was once a terminal section of track which ran from Darwin into the interior to the outpost of Birdum. However, an extremely violent tropical hurricane damaged the line and it was never put back in service, unlike the famous Key West line in Florida.

BLUE TRAIN

"One of the most important episodes in the history of maritime exploration – the discovery 500 years ago of the Cape of Good Hope by the Portuguese seaman Bartolomeo Diaz – was celebrated by his contemporary Luis Camões, who in the reign of Philip II wrote an epic glorifying these early navigators, just as Virgil had sung the glories of the Latin seamen in the *Aeneid* 1,500 years earlier." This debatable parallel appeared in the pages of *Momentum*, the glossy, two-language (English and Afrikaans) company magazine of the SAA – the

society responsible for handling almost all transport in the Republic of South Africa, including the railways. The frontispiece illustrates the spanner with which President Kruger, on 2 November 1894, tightened the last bolt of the Pretoria–Cape Town line. This is the line travelled by the Blue Train, the most luxurious in the world. The magazine also points out, quite apart from the usual publicity clichés, the merits of the train. It emphasizes the luxury of the single cars resembling mini-apartments with private showers, and lists the splendid dishes served in the restaurant car. The train's timetable allows 25 hours to cover the 1,000 miles (1,600 km) between the two cities, descending from the 5,575 ft (1,700 m) of the Transvaal highlands to sea level. Departures from the two stations take place several times a week according to an elaborate calendar which is more like a maritime guidebook than a railway timetable. If you choose one of the wrong days, you will have to put up with the more ordinary Trans-Karoo.

The part of Africa the Blue Train crosses has a pleasant climate, where the fauna and flora are strictly protected and you can almost imagine yourself in a terrestrial paradise. From the windows of the luxury compartments a variety of landscapes succeeds another: savannas and forests, dark mountains streaked with veins of rich minerals, and deserts which fringe the Atlantic. There are also villages in the Dutch colonial style surrounded by gentle hills covered with vines, reminiscent of the vineyards of Europe.

Departure from Pretoria is early in the morning and the train is scheduled to arrive in Cape Town just before midday of the following day. Apartheid has recently been abolished on public transport. No longer is it possible for a non-white to be insulted as

In 1985 the SAA celebrated its 75th anniversary. This company manages much of the Republic of South Africa's transport system, not only the railways but also road services and the country's largest fleet of airliners. South Africa vies with Australia and the Soviet Union for the longest goods trains, some of which are several kilometers in length.
Opposite: The engine of the Blue Train moves out from the shadow of Johannesburg's skyscrapers, pulling what is perhaps the most luxurious train in the world. The cars are veritable suites with such amenities as showers and double beds. The gauge, as is the case throughout southern Africa, is narrow (1,065 mm).

was the young lawyer Gandhi who was thrown out of the first-class carriage because he was Indian. The regular passengers include diplomats, civil servants and government officials who commute between the cities, each of which takes turns in functioning as capital. Some of them disdain the frequent air shuttles which link the two ends of the country in a couple of hours; the famous train is doubtless something of a status symbol – and costs more than the air flight.

Pretoria station is within sight of the museum of Paul Kruger, the president who was the symbol of heroic Boer resistance to British infiltration. In the garden is the railway car which served him as a travelling platform where he held his meetings and from which he made his speeches.

The express finally proceeds to Johannesburg. The yellow paintwork of the first-class carriages becomes lost in the profusion of flowering trees. The country's financial metropolis was linked with the capital by the Metroblitz Jakaranda, the famous train whose name was derived from the spring flowers which bloom so profusely but briefly along the city avenues.

The train enters a tunnel, in part using those which once led to the diamond mines and which nowadays carry commuter traffic direct to the city suburbs. The users of the trains on the intersecting lines from Soweto and elsewhere are mostly black.

In the afternoon the Blue Train crosses the vast plain of the Vaal. At Warrenton there are, in theory, connections to the north. The South African rail network is linked, thanks to a common gauge of 1,065 mm (the so-called "Cape gauge") with all the neighbouring countries. You can therefore take a train to Botswana, Zimbabwe, Mozambique, Malawi, Zambia and even

Zaïre, unless temporarily strained relations with some of the governments concerned make such journeys inadvisable. A little further on the train stops at Kimberley, the city which used to symbolize diamond production – now concentrated elsewhere – which played a key role in the Republic's economic good fortune. Not far from the town is the "big hole," an awesome precipice excavated by intensive mining which contained the priceless stones now displayed in museum cases or owned by the world's rulers.

Kimberley is the geographic center of the nation, as it was once its economic and financial heart. It is also a stop for the other famous South African train, the Trans-Oranje, which links Durban to Cape Town in 37 hours. The route follows a broad horseshoe loop since there is at present no direct coastal service along the Indian Ocean. Before night falls it stops at De Aar, departure point for the very long rail link with Namibia. It is 878 miles (1,415 km) to the capital, Windhoek, served by an express named Suidwester which skirts the Kalahari Desert. The place name is clearly Dutch, in contrast to the appearance of the station, which is reminiscent of certain smart little Saxon stations in what was formerly Saxe-Coburg, now dismantled and out of service as a result of the post-war division of Germany.

Morning dawns on a landscape scored with rows of vineyards standing out against the outline of the majestic mountains. The train continues its journey beneath this unique mountain chain – long, straight and level. We are at the Cape, with its delightful setting and the unmistakable outline of Table Mountain looming over it.

This mountain seems to have been placed there to protect one of the most spectacular cities in the world.

Cape Town – Kaapstad in the Boer version – is set among green hills. In the background the Table Mountain Cableway – a suspended thread of wire which seems to be a continuation of the railway line – is silhouetted against mossy outcrops of rock and leads up to a marvellous lookout point. At the top, signs point towards the furthest corners of the southern hemisphere, to Perth, Buenos Aires and Antarctica as though it were possible to see them.

The Cape is a riot of colours and flowers growing beneath the dappled shade of oaks and dominated by the queen of local flora, the protea. Linnaeus, although unaware of its changing appearance (there are over 100 species), chose this name derived from a mythical Mediterranean god who had the power to adopt the most varied guises. There are many other plants which also seem to have survived from a classical age and have taken on Greek names that describe their almost mythical beauty: agapanthus, crassula, helichrysum, oxalis and pelargonium.

CHAPTER 5

A TRAIN FOR ALL SEASONS

134

At Peterborough, not far from Cambridge, England, the Thomas Cook railway timetables are printed. Two editions appear every month, one red and one blue. The red book covers all the countries in Europe; the blue covers the rest of the world.

Unlike the more familiar ABC air timetables – another famed British institution – which every travel agent has to hand, the Thomas Cook volumes tend to be little known abroad. This is a pity because they are genuine mines of information on methods of transport that are usually forgotten, not only trains but also buses, ferries and even trucks used for passenger services.

It is therefore possible to plan down to the last detail a journey, for example, across the Sahara desert or the icefields of the Yukon, including exact distances and prices. The timetables show that the train is well adapted to a broad range of climatic conditions in countries widely separated from one another, from overpopulated Japan to underdeveloped and semidesert Mali.

Yet railways, whether they be classified as metropolitan, underground, funicular or rack-and-pinion, perform a much more significant role. They enable the inhabitants of huge urban areas to move about freely and provide access to otherwise inaccessible mountain destinations.

It is thus conceivable to talk about a train for all seasons, if we look at it from an economic and political viewpoint. Naturally every government has attempted to mould the railways to its own ends, from time to time making it either an instrument of propaganda or of territorial planning.

Yet a means of transport is not merely a neutral instrument. Apart from the technical features which militate for or against a particular type of traffic, there are often considerations of a more general character which help to determine the choice. And in this sense the timetables represent a valuable source of information over and above the essential needs of the traveller.

Absurd as it may seem, it is not always easy to obtain information on the spot, either because of bureaucratic inefficiency of even because certain governments see it as a security risk. All credit, therefore, to the editors of Thomas Cook for obtaining all the daily information that is essential to governments the world over.

THE TRAIN AS LIBERATOR

When railway services are introduced into remote areas, they are welcomed by the local people with overwhelming gratitude for the arrival of a means of transport destined to end their years of isolation. Such a sentiment pervaded the whole of Europe in the second half of the nineteenth century: it was particularly strong in the rural communities which suffered more from being situated at such a distance from the principal centers of production and culture.

However, the association between the train and freedom was nowhere more evident than in America where the epic conquest of the West was sealed by the advance of the railroads in the wake of the pioneers' covered wagons. This had a lasting effect on the history of this great country which was still in its early stages. Just as the train initially personified the yearning for new frontiers, it later came to be seen as the opportunity for escape from the unemployment and poverty of the Depression years. It was the salvation of the generation which abandoned the dusty towns of the prairie for the Californian mirage, whose plight was recounted in the songs of Woody Guthrie.

It was the train, too, which produced those strange and colourful folk known as "hobos," harmless vagrants who prefer life along the track, waiting for the chance to hide in a goods car and travel free from coast to coast. Freedom was also the goal of clandestine immigrants from Mexico, though it was a tragic illusion for some who were found dead of thirst in an empty carriage on a sunbaked Texan siding in the summer of 1987. Dramatic incidents such as these have been known, too, on the other side of the world, where dictatorships have tried to clamp down on waves of

Below: a print of the Grand Trunk Railway of Canada dating from the late nineteenth century.
On the previous page: A train of the Rhaetian Railways among the glaciers of the Bernina. Many trains were designed principally for VIPs, every detail proclaiming the authority of the illustrious passenger in question.

RAND AVERY SUPPLY CO., BOSTON.   1896

illegal immigration from underdeveloped countries.

Despite the upheavals of the terrible years of the Second World War, very different emotions were aroused by the trains of the liberators, as can be seen in the photographs showing the first Allied train to enter Rome's Termini station in June 1944.

The same scenes were repeated a year later at Tutuban station in Manila, the day on which General MacArthur kept his promise to the Filipinos that he would return there victorious against the Japanese invaders.

Although they would never admit to it, governments often promote their own causes by transforming the so-called "freedom trains" into "people's trains." This has happened almost invariably in the aftermath of modern revolutions, when the avenging heroes of injustice don the clothes of government officials. All this would take place amidst great celebrations.

In 1985, while the railways of the German Federal Republic were commemorating 150 years since the opening of the first German line (the Nuremberg–Furth in Bavaria), their counterparts in the German Democratic Republic took the opportunity of celebrating the first 40 years of their railways "in the hands of the people."

At Monastir there is a large station in white marble. This is not some relic of the colonial past. The train made its appearance in this elegant seaside resort only a few years ago, when the Tunisian government showed renewed interest in the country's railways. There was of course a motive behind such magnificent architecture: Monastir is the birthplace of Habib Bourghiba. Just before he was deposed, the old patriarch had the satisfaction of opening a prestigious building which

Left and below: The train of Pope Pius IX, photographed in 1951.

would mean that future citizens would remember him better. Street names or equestrian monuments do not have such impact.

Naturally the proud tradition of great civic enterprises goes back to the beginnings of civilization. By exalting the position of the train, governments are simply evoking this tradition. Often it is hard to distinguish between undertakings that are of real practical advantage, which are subsequently ascribed to the political merits of this or that government, and vainglorious constructions that are no more than self-dedicated monuments to the men who control the purse-strings.

In Italy the train was instrumental in giving Fascism a respectable image in the eyes of the middle classes. After the First World War the "black shirts" took over the running of the trains from striking engineers. Their efficiency was renowned and anyone recalling the years of Fascist rule to this day will invariably talk of how the trains never failed to run on time under this arrangement. However, the Fascist regime never acknowledged its debt to the railways by promoting further construction. In Libya, then under Italian rule, priority was given to the construction of the Via Balba, the coastal road linking Tripoli and Benghazi, while in the built-up areas there were already plans in operation to suppress secondary lines. It was an unmistakable sign of the growing influence of the automobile industry which to a certain extent undermined the importance of the railways.

THE TRAIN TO TOWN

Often late, always crowded, sometimes cancelled. Perhaps these descriptions summarize the reaction of many people to the train that takes them to and from work each day. If we had to travel in the conditions of a century ago, however, such drawbacks would seem mild. Passengers in the second class probably had a roof over their heads but the sides of the carriage were often open, exposed to the weather. Third-class carriages had no roof and the only concession to the weather might be holes drilled in the floor to allow rain to drain away. Third-class carriages on the London and Greenwich Railway in 1836 had no seats. On the London and Southampton Railway in 1838 the third-class carriages were open flat trucks with movable garden seats placed on them. In 1844 Parliament decreed that third-class carriages should be protected from the weather and fitted with seats. Railways were to provide at least one train daily in each direction with third-class accommodation, and each such train was to call at all stations on the line while maintaining an average speed not less than 12 mph (19 kmh). Fares were not to exceed one penny a mile.

The railways disliked these conditions and tended to run their "Parliamentary Trains" at inconvenient times. More remunerative traffic was calculated to be among prosperous businessmen who commuted to the City of London from their residences on the coast or in the country. Season tickets from Brighton to London were issued by the London, Brighton and South Coast Railway in 1845 and were available to first-class travellers only. Fast trains with first-class carriages only were run between Brighton and London Bridge.

The 8.45 a.m. to London and 5 p.m. return trains were accelerated over the years. In 1867 Pullman cars appeared on the train and in 1907 it was officially named The City Limited. Third-class passengers were not conveyed until 1919. Second class in Britain at that time was confined to certain Continental services and was virtually indistinguishable from third. In the 1850s, however, all three classes were available on the Brighton line. A notice in the company's timetable announced that there would be no second-class carriages on the morning and evening fast business trains "except for servants travelling with their employers."

A long walk to work was accepted by many less exalted persons but in some cases this beneficial exercise was impracticable because railway building in the capital had necessitated the destruction of many houses, whose occupants had to move further out. In 1854 the Great Eastern Railway was obliged by an Act of Parliament to convey workers from Edmonton and Walthamstow in north-east London to its Bishopsgate terminus in east London for a return fare of twopence. The resultant boom in traffic soon overtaxed the station at Bishopsgate and led to the move to Liverpool Street, now one of London's most famous and busy stations. A similar situation arose in 1865 when the London, Chatham and Dover Railway built a line from Ludgate Hill through south London to Victoria station. The company began running two trains daily over the route in each direction for "the exclusive accommodation of artisans, mechanics and daily labourers, of both sexes, going to their work or returning to their houses."

In 1868 an Act of Parliament recommended that all railways running out of London should provide transport at the

Opposite: Two posters for the Ferrovie Nord, Milan, in the fifties, when this network was not yet mainly associated with commuter traffic and still attempted to encourage tourists to use trains for short fishing trips or day trips to the countryside.
Above: A railwayman's cap bearing the insignia of the Ferrovie Nord.

rate of one penny for seven or eight miles. The ruling was enforced at the discretion of the Board of Trade and some railways were ingenious in finding excuses for evading it. Workers often walked long distances to a station where cheap fares were in operation.

Steam working of intensive suburban services reached its climax at Liverpool Street on the Great Eastern Railway in 1920 when in peak periods a train entered each platform every ten minutes and 51 trains left the terminus between 5 p.m. and 6 p.m. Extra engine spurs were laid, on which locomotives could wait to take over arriving trains and work them back to the suburbs. This was long before the days of push-button signalling and the physical work for the signalmen in operating signals and changing points must have been considerable.

Although some railways held out against electrification the convenience of a train that occupied a platform at a terminus for no longer than it took the driver to walk from one end to the other was obvious. The multiple-unit electric suburban train owes its development to Frank J. Sprague in the United States. In his system the driver in the leading cab of an electric train could control all the motors in the train from his master controller. A train might be composed of units of four coaches, with motors on the front and rear coaches. The units could be coupled together to form trains of eight or 12 coaches according to the traffic demand, and because the number of motors increased in proportion to the length of the train, there was no falling off in performance, as there was when extra coaches were added to a train hauled by a steam locomotive. The multiple-unit system of working soon became universal on suburban lines. Sprague's first successful

application of his system on a railway line was in 1897 on the South Side elevated line in Chicago.

The first suburban railway to be electrified in the United States was the North shore Railroad in California in 1903. The line connected with ferries to San Francisco and replaced a previous narrow-gauge steam line which had been built to serve growing residential districts north of the bay. The first major commuter railroad to electrify its service was the Long Island Railroad which made the changeover from steam in 1905. The line was practically crippled by its intensive traffic during the Second World War and in 1949 was bankrupt. A rehabilitation programme undertaken by the Pennsylvania Railroad equipped it with double-deck coaches. When the Pennsylvania Railroad succumbed to financial problems, further rehabilitation was undertaken in 1965 by the Metropolitan Transport Authority of New York. Among the improvements were new trains capable of 100 mph (160 kmh).

Less exclusive than supplementary fare services are the City-Bahn trains operated by the German Federal Railway between the centers of some large cities and their suburbs. The first City-Bahn train was introduced between Cologne and Gummersbach in 1984. One compartment between the first- and second-class sections of a City-Bahn train is equipped with automatic machines dispensing hot and cold drinks. There are no seats but upholstered backrests round a central table provide a little comfort and stability while standing up.

Where does one begin to distinguish between a suburban line and a main line? In England the Metropolitan Railway extended from London into Hertfordshire

Almost half the Swiss railway network is run by private companies. Altogether these private lines have 1,261 miles (2,031 km) of track, with 1,049 stations and 8,117 employees. In contrast, the federal network (SBB) has 1,854 miles (2,986 km) of track, 811 stations and about 36,970 employees. The traffic generated by the state network is more than double that of the private companies. Yet the whole Swiss system is perfectly integrated, even when it comes to fares.
Below: A train of the Rhaetian Railways on its way to Davos Glaris.
Opposite: A glimpse of the interior of the French presidential train, used by Albert Lebrun for his visit to London in 1939.

and Buckinghamshire, encouraging house building around existing small towns and creating what it called "Metroland." It liked to think of itself as a main line and provided a Pullman car on certain morning and evening trains to and from the city. The Long Island Railroad in the United States penetrated still further into the country. It is 115 miles (185 km) from New York City to Montauk at the tip of Long Island. Montauk commuters can pay a supplement for a "Red Carpet" service in one of the "Sunrise fleet" of parlour cars with armchair seating and stewards serving refreshments. A two-tier supplement system was introduced soon after the service began and a disparity showed up between travel in the two directions. Weary executives travelling home after a bruising day in

141

the city were readier to patronize the service than when travelling inwards full of optimism and energy in the morning and capable of withstanding the rigours of travelling with the generality of office workers. They were enticed to the Red Carpet by a lower supplement for the journey into New York.

Perhaps more steps to make commuting as comfortable as possible will be taken in future and some who are tired of driving to work through ever-increasing traffic jams may be prepared to pay a supplement and return to the train to town. For the railways commuter traffic remains an economic problem. Providing a large fleet of vehicles that is only fully utilized at peak periods seems destined always to incur expenditure that outweighs additional revenue.

Opposite and below: Two pictures of railway lines in Sardinia, one showing an engine pulling a coach along the jetty at Artabax, the other a railcar crossing a high viaduct.

PRIVATE AND NATIONALIZED SERVICES

An elderly gentleman smiles complacently as he stands in front of a perfectly restored carriage bearing the insignia of the Texas Mexican Railway. The American magazine which devotes a whole report to Andrés Ramos and his railway proclaims triumphantly: "This train runs for the money." The article explains that the Tex Mex Express is not just the whim of an enthusiast, nor a rare social initiative in the realm of American transport, nor even an example of historic restoration.

The fact is simply that after several decades a private entrepreneur decided to revive the adventure of passenger travel, convinced that he could make a profit from it. So he created an intercity service between Laredo and Corpus Christi, on the Gulf of Mexico, along the tracks of a railway line that he already owned, running parallel to the border, and which since 1946 had carried only goods traffic. With this advantage to hand, Mr Ramos has demonstrated that with modest investment and by reconverting part of the rolling stock for new traffic, the venture could be profitable.

In the Old World, however, all the efforts of those far-sighted private Swiss companies which run almost half the country's rail system, including the spectacular mountain trains, have not proved enough to upset deep-rooted traditions. Examination of the balance sheets reveals that some of them operate at a profit but only because they can boast an almost exclusive monopoly in providing services to the famous ski resorts.

One example is the Brig–Visp–Zermatt, with lines up the Jungfrau and the Rigi, both of which attract tourists from all over

the world, who pay high prices to visit them and to spend holidays in the vicinity. Another is the BLS, the Lötschberg, without alternative routes for a radius of over 65 miles (100 km). But to carry out the extremely expensive work of doubling the line on the southern stretch, along the scenic descent of the Vallese, it has proved essential to obtain federal financial help. And public money is needed to subsidize other private enterprises, notably the Rhaetian Railways to the Furka-Oberalp, to make good the inevitable deficit incurred by an undertaking which demanded rigorous and dynamic management.

Private ownership of railways, and their successful management under this arrangement, remains a controversial issue. In

Sardinian lines are impressively long; that linking Cagliari to Artabax is 142 miles (228 km) long, and that linking Sassari to Palau 93 miles (150 km) long. Another scenic line is the Mandas–Sorgono branch (60 miles/97 km), admired by, among others, D. H. Lawrence.

Spain, for example, the regional lines of Catalonia were managed by private operators until the 1970s, but had it not been for the subsequent intervention of the Generalitat, namely the autonomous government, the Monserrat train would today just be a memory, given the increasing obsolescence by then of the rolling stock and the fixed installations.

Socialists will continue to argue that private ownership of stations and lines is undesirable, and that public transport fulfils an essential need in society that transcends profit. Yet today, as never before, there is an increasing trend in the West towards denationalization. The champions of deregulation and privatization are inevitably as dogmatic in their views as their opponents who favour state ownership. No doubt the argument will rage on, to be solved in time by whichever method is the most efficient and cost-effective, and the one more likely to create sufficient investment for the maintenance, development, and thus survival of the railways.

Many railways the world over are operating at a massive deficit, often resulting in the suspension of certain services, and the closure of favourite local lines, often those very lines that had in the past liberated the inhabitants of remote areas by providing them with a much-needed transport link. The truth is that the train's natural enemy is the motor car. The increased popularity of private motoring throughout the twentieth century has inevitably eroded public transport, reducing the train to a position of secondary importance. As things stand now, the railways are, with rare exceptions, doomed to lose money and thus to require some measure of public support. Future developments should be interesting to monitor.

The Ferrovie Nord, Milan, is of prime importance from the viewpoint of European commuter traffic. *Above: Detail of one of its diesel locomotives.*

EXOTIC, TROPICAL AND ARCTIC TRAINS

With a view to persuading some of the holiday-makers attracted by the reduced fares of the "Nouvelles Frontières" agency to stay in France, rather than holiday abroad, the French railways have launched a series of panoramic trains with vaguely exotic names such as Le Cevenol and Le Paludier, provided with films, hostesses in regional costume and other attractions. This is an example of how the train can successfully be harnessed as an instrument of luxury, promising exoticism and adventure. Rail travel, after all, has a romantic and glamorous tradition, and there has been a revival of interest in this more leisurely aspect, turning the journey itself into an integral part of a holiday rather than simply the mundane means of reaching a holiday destination. The romance of the great train journeys of the world is still very much alive.

To find truly "tropical" trains you must go to Cuba, where you can travel on the ancient Hershey electric trains of the coast line to Mastanzas, or to neighbouring Jamaica where, in just $5\frac{1}{2}$ hours, you cross the island from Kingston to Montego Bay. Among giant palms and terraced ricefields, the Singhalese trains clatter alarmingly down from Kandy to Colombo, although they are far safer than the old Leyland buses shot at repeatedly by rebel Tamils.

The trains that cross the great deserts have a subtle charm of their own; they include the Suidwester, or Namibia Express, and the trains for Tozeur which literally exist for the benefit of the mineral oases of southern Tunisia.

The acme of exoticism, however, is to be found in Latin America, especially in the Bolivian highlands, when, having left La

Paz (at an altitude of more than 13,100 ft (4,000 m), the train, its wooden coaches crowded with Indians in coloured ponchos, climbs even higher, leaving the capital, with its huts and skyscrapers, far below. And in Ecuador the old "coffeepots," which are still in service, appear appropriately as the trademark of a brand of coffee. As counterparts to these high-altitude lines there are those that run through the earth's natural depressions, such as the new Israeli line to Sedom (the nefarious Sodom of the Bible), along the shores of the Dead Sea, at 985 ft (300 m) and more below sea level.

The record for slowness is probably held by a very narrow-gauge (0.60 cm) railway of northern Zaire, the Isiro–Aketi, which takes 37 hours to travel 347 miles (559 km) through the heart of virgin forest.

Exotic trains such as these are not necessarily exposed only to scorching heat. The train, often electric, and necessarily furnished with powerful snowploughs and heaters, can also adapt itself to intense cold. Again, without venturing too far afield, a short trip in January through the Swiss Jura, for instance on the Le Pont–Le Brassus line, can be comparable to a Siberian adventure.

There are, of course, the railways of the Far North, such as the Leningrad–Murmansk, which take Russian passengers to the shores of the Arctic Ocean, permanently ice-free because of the warm Gulf currents. Or the Trondheim–Bodo, on which the courteous and attentive Norwegian guards assign you seats like in a theater and give every passenger an adhesive label bearing the legend: "I have crossed the Polar Circle. In Norway, by train." Or the Helsinki–Rovaniemi, where passengers can savour the view of some of the 15,000 Finnish lakes in the background.

A picture of the Zigzag Railway in the Blue Mountains of New South Wales. This is a truly exotic train, not only because of its location but also because it is run with ancient rolling stock for the delight of Australian and foreign tourists.

North America, too, boasts its arctic trains, like the Polar Bear Express and the Hudson Bay to the remote Canadian outpost of Churchill. Or the Aurora which runs from Anchorage through the heart of Alaska to Fairbanks. Also worthy of a mention is Skagway–Whitehorse – unfortunately closed some years ago because of the high cost of keeping the line free of ice, but now partially reopened – which had its moment of glory at the time of the Klondike gold rush.

The modern counterparts of those gold prospectors are peaceful tourists on their way to visit the Mount McKinley national park and to photograph elks and brown bears – naturally, from the train windows.

TRAIN LINKS WITH SEA AND AIR

Boat trains are of immense importance in maintaining efficient transport links between countries, either connecting with ferry services or, in some cases, boarding the ferry directly. The boats that travel between Germany, Denmark and Sweden are well known, and a great volume of "mixed" traffic, between Britain and the Continent, with transshipment on the quays, is recorded at all the main Channel ports. The last direct coach from Paris to London, the wagon-lit attached to the night ferry, was removed from service some years ago.

Time was when the Tsarist nobility would board the Nord Express at St Petersburg bound for the French capital and then the Sud Express to Lisbon, thus gaining several days' sailing time to America. Road and air links have made this kind of time-saving exercise redundant.

Unlike the automobile, other means of transport, aware of their limitations, have

Below: Postcard reproducing a poster of 1919 advertising the service from London to Southend, a port in the Thames estuary.
Opposite: A splendid aerial view of Venice, with the main-line station of Santa Lucia in the foreground, blending perfectly into the townscape.

SOUTHEND *BY* DISTRICT RAILWAY THROUGH TRAINS

to be satisfied with coming as near as possible. Where one is not available, another will be there to take the traveller to his or her destination. From Austria to Norway it is usual to alight from a tram and board a boat or train and finally a coach, travelling on a single ticket and with very convenient connections.

Only the automobile is basically self-reliant, enabling you to go anywhere, seated behind the steering-wheel, although only the most stupid individual would consider paving over Venice's Grand Canal – plans to do this have actually been published – in order to be able to park your car in St Mark's Square. Re-educating people on the more rational use of various forms of transport, after the hysteria generated by motoring, is probably one of the basic tasks that countries have to tackle in the years to come.

An important contribution in this respect is the expansion of rail links to airports, as has recently happened in Europe, America and Japan. Usually this is a special line, with frequent shuttle services, to and from the city centers, as in Barcelona, Brussels and Paris. Elsewhere underground lines connect directly with airports, as at Chicago, Washington DC and London's Heathrow. Tokyo Haneda can be reached by monorail.

However, by far the best solution is that adopted at Zurich, Geneva, Frankfurt and Amsterdam, where the airport is connected with dozens of express trains which run regularly to all nearby towns within a radius of 125–185 miles (200–300 km). In Switzerland it has become normal to start a journey to foreign capitals or tropical beaches from the nearest railway station, where there will certainly be a direct service to Kloten (Zurich) or Cointrin (Geneva) and where you can check in your

baggage without any further worry as far as Reykjavik or Malindi.

When civil aviation began its dizzy climb to success, the fate of the train appeared to be sealed. It was believed that nobody would use it any more, when boarding an aircraft was as easy as getting on to a bus. Later it was realized that a one-hour flight meant spending twice as much time on the ground in order to travel to and from the terminals in city traffic.

In order to achieve the ultimate in speed and comfort – debatable, in any event, for middle distance since the advent of high-speed trains – the airlines have had to resort for assistance to the trusty old railways.

UNDERGROUND AND CITY TRAINS

Although only third in chronological order, being opened in 1900, after London and Budapest, the Paris underground railway is one of the attractions of the *ville lumière*, like the Seine and the Eiffel Tower. Since it is a genuine urban network, it is deeply rooted in the Parisian lifestyle. Its stations are close together, their distinctive Art Nouveau entrances by Hector Guimard located in the center of the various quarters. Until a few years ago the lines ended at the city gates, so that there was a clear demarcation between the metropolis and the suburbs. But because of the steady expansion of the city, which today comprises much of the Île de France, it was found necessary to build a new super-metropolitan, the RER (Réseau Express Régional), running below the existing one and carrying passengers in a matter of minutes from the Bois de Vincennes to La Défense.

Such duplication is not needed in London, where the underground or "tube," as

A shuttle train of the DB photographed at Frankfurt Airport (Europe's second-busiest), which runs directly underneath the runways. The idea of a train link to the air terminal is most effective. Not only do the shuttles run to and from the city center in a few minutes, but many intercity trains also provide a service, so that passengers throughout central Germany have easy access to the airport.

Opposite: An innovative experimental train, Pittsburgh, 1966. This type of enterprise has not always met with the approval of local citizens and administrators. The old industrial metropolis of Pennsylvania subsequently abandoned this project, preferring to modernize the trolley-car system instead.

it is commonly known, consisting of streamlined carriages which almost seem to stick to the tunnel walls, was planned on a regional basis, so that even in Victorian times it extended in all directions from the center of what was then the largest city in the world.

Yet in terms of size neither of these systems compares with the New York "subway," with 230 miles (370 km) of line and 462 stations, open throughout the day and night, and the only one to boast four-track lines with express and local trains. It also has a sinister reputation as a place where all manner of criminal activities can occur. The American media have so highlighted the terrors of this subterranean jungle (sensations reinforced by innumerable films) that the authorities of other cities have for some time looked askance at any plans for new underground systems; having realized the inadequacy of the "freeways" to solve traffic problems, they have taken exceptional measures on their new trains to avoid a repetition of this sorry state of events. The most recent networks, like those in San Francisco, Washington DC, Baltimore and Atlanta, are spotlessly clean, while in Miami you risk being arrested if you are caught nibbling a sandwich inside the car. The difference is underlined by the names; thus "subway" remains unique to New York, while the others are "rapid transit" or simply "metro."

But neither in Paris, nor in London, nor in New York is the volume of traffic equal to that in the Far East, where the metropolitan lines of Tokyo, Osaka, Seoul and Hong Kong, hastily developed in a few years with a speed that would be inconceivable in the West, represent prime examples of technological efficiency in the public sector.

However, no network, including those

of Asia, can compare in magnificence and grandeur with the Moscow metro, with its impressive marble stairways and its theatrical chandeliers, built by Stalin and his successors as a permanent glorification of the regime.

Basically, every underground system, apart from constituting a complex organization, often superior to some national railway companies, mirrors the habits, vices and virtues – indeed the whole character – of society in the world above. To travel on lines 6 and 8 of the Berlin "Ubahn," on trains which pass through shadowy stations located to the east of the Wall, with dusty signs that hark back to the days of the Third Reich, one can understand, better than by reading weighty tomes, the drama of the former capital, until recently split in half.

To experience the atmosphere of any

The complex topography of London's underground system (below) and of the Paris métro (opposite) has been reproduced in many forms, on postcards, T-shirts etc. In fact, it is not easy for newcomers to these cities to find their way around these mazes. The métro retains its Art Nouveau features, still recognizable in some of the older entrances which have been lovingly restored. In New York entries to the subway are often located inside skyscrapers or office complexes.

city you have to venture down into its underground system. If the rush hours are avoided, a journey can hold many surprises in store, from the style and fittings of the stations (sometimes, as in Marseilles or Prague, highly original), to veritable subterranean museums, as on some levels in Mexico City, where the lost monuments of Aztec civilization have been reconstructed.

The elevated trains, too, previously condemned as noisy and ugly, after the unhappy experience of Chicago's loop, are staging a comeback, especially as they are cheaper to run. Miami, for example, has opted for a train on stilts which runs from north to south, rather than risk excavating the soft, sandy soil of southern Florida.

The enormous investment cost involved is virtually the only drawback to the proliferation of underground lines which by now are operating in cities as far apart as Peking and Santiago, Stockholm and Calcutta. But it is still a powerful argument for keeping another type of urban railway system which seemed doomed to extinction.

Contrary to what is sometimes believed, the tram is not necessarily older than the underground train. When trains were already running below London, electric trams had not yet been invented. Nor are they inevitably slower. The Red Arrows, which are capable of reaching 75 mph (120 kmh) still serve the outskirts of Philadelphia. Furthermore, trams are not noisier than buses, provided the brake system and the rails are kept in good shape, and they certainly cause less pollution.

Nevertheless it is the tram, more than any other means of transport, which has suffered many attacks and calumnies. It is the most nostalgically loved means of transport for that romantic appeal which no underground can possess, and also the

150

UNDERGROUND

©Copyright London Underground Limited

most hated, for the simple reason that it often usurps the space considered to belong to the motorist, who has become lord, if not tyrant, of the roads.

These considerations account for the extraordinary rise of tram systems in the first quarter of the present century, with the multiplication of lines even in provincial towns – not to mention the hundreds of American networks, their streetcars immortalized in the films of Laurel and Hardy – and their equally rapid decline after the Second World War.

In Paris the last tram was taken out of service in 1937. After the war the unions of other French cities unthinkingly agreed to follow the example of the capital, with the sole exception of St Etienne, where an excellent tramway, duly modernized, still provides a first-class service for the city. This coal-mining town in the Massif Central always seems to swim against the current, in politics, in sport and, as here, in transport. But as a result of its obstinacy, the tram duly made a grand-style comeback in Nice and Grenoble; maybe some day it will return to Paris itself.

The same applies to Spain, where the last tram vanished from the scene in 1976, except for a couple of tourist tracks in Barcelona and on the island of Majorca. Italian closures, recently decreed in cities such as Genoa, Trieste and Cagliari, have proved to be bitterly regretted blunders. Rome phased out its trams in 1960, when it acted as host to the Olympic Games, a decision which many believe was directly responsible for the present chaotic management of the city's public transport system. After many vicissitudes, the only tram networks to be saved in Italy were those of Milan and Turin.

Things were somewhat different in Germany, Austria, Switzerland, Belgium and

Holland, and in certain isolated places such as Göteborg, Helsinki, Toronto and Melbourne, where a sensible policy of tramway modernization has helped to maintain mass support for this form of public transport. In eastern Europe trams are universally popular, continuously on the increase and operating in about 180 cities from Leipzig to Vladivostok and from Sofia to Leningrad, which boasts the most extensive network in the world.

Today the tram, although usually known as "light rail," is making headway almost everywhere. Even the legendary Silicon Valley of California is nowadays served by ultra-modern trams, while the world capital of the automobile, Detroit, after purchasing some ancient models from

151

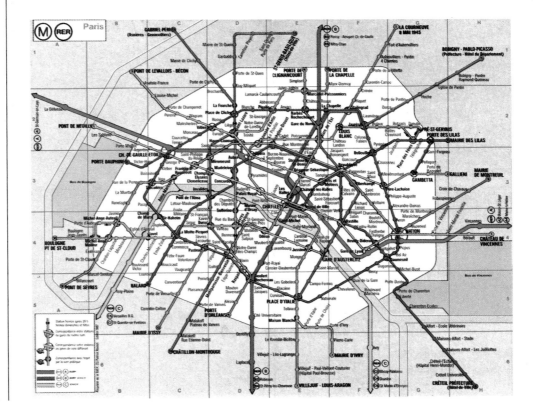

For many people, commuting by train has become part of their daily routine. Without commuter rail networks, capable of transporting hundreds of thousands of people every day into large cities from the surrounding areas, the industrial and commercial development of many countries during the twentieth century would have been unthinkable.

Opposite: The elevated railway above the streets of Manhattan, subsequently removed to make way for new buildings. In the United States only Chicago still has a line of this kind (the so-called "loop") which surrounds the business quarters. *Opposite:* A cable trolley from Denver and the symbol of the Pacific Electric, which managed the suburban lines of Los Angeles.

Oporto to give its downtown area a touch of frivolity, has introduced a "people mover" which bustles around in the shadow of the city skyscrapers.

With a few picturesque exceptions – the *eletricos* of Lisbon, the antediluvian street-cars of Hanoi and the horse-trams that delight tourists in Douglas on the Isle of Man – the sector is notable for its technological progress. In London, an elevated tramway was opted for as part of the plan for revitalizing the Docklands area. This does not, however, imply the return of the "double deckers," now to be seen only among the skyscrapers of the business district of Hong Kong and, to give a single example, along the seafront of Blackpool.

The comeback of the tram was still unthinkable at the beginning of the 1970s, when the duel between rails and rubber tyres in towns seemed to have been finally settled in favour of the buses. Today we do not know whether trams will make a full comeback, but one thing is certain, cars will have to be kept out of many major city centers.

HILL AND MOUNTAIN TRAINS

The Swiss have modernized virtually all of their mountain railway installations, so that their loveliest valleys can be enjoyed to the full. They have made not only a shrewd economic investment but have also created a process of popular tourism whereby family groups and elderly people can travel up mountains to reach peaks that would otherwise be accessible only to a few expert climbers. And it has all been achieved whilst taking the utmost care of the environment, which would certainly have been polluted by mass motoring.

Many people believe that the need to

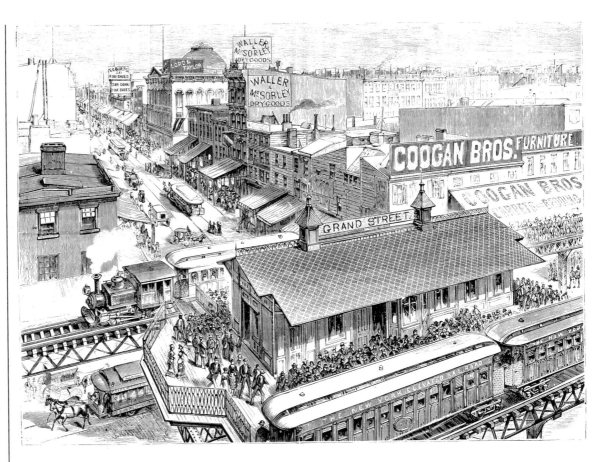

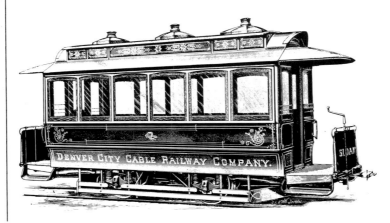

overcome marked differences in height must constitute an insuperable handicap for a railway. This is only partly true because although with normal traction trains can only climb fairly gentle slopes (the record, for standard-gauge, is on the Uetliberg line above Zurich, with a gradient of 70 per thousand; and for metric-gauge, on the Trogenerbahn, near St Gallen, with 75 per thousand), with the aid of artificial mechanisms they can get to the top of otherwise inaccessible peaks. The most daring cogwheel line is that of Pilatus, above Lucerne, with gradients of 480 per thousand. The carriages are hauled up by means of a cog attached to a wheel situated in the centre of the traditional track. This wheel may be fixed, as in this instance, or mobile, as on the nearby Engelberg line, where the cogwheel train operates only over the steepest parts of the route. In the second case, the vehicles look exactly like normal trains, with the same type of locomotive and carriages as those of the Federal Railways which run from Lucerne to Interlaken by way of the Brunig.

In the case of funiculars – which use rails but with the cabins drawn up and down by a cable – the gradient record is also held by Switzerland. The Piotta–Ritòm reaches 878 per thousand, only a little less than that of a lift. The Swiss have more than 50 funiculars in service (another world record), and more than 27 partial or entire cogwheel lines, more than one third of the global total. Moreover, Swiss factories manufacture most of the rolling stock destined for other countries, including the United States.

Where exactly does this specialized form of transport fit into the railway sector as a whole? Should we include, in addition to the simple, suspension type of funicular, the multiple variations in the shape of cable-cars, chair-lifts and ski-lifts? Some would rule them out because they do not depend on a train.

Apart from the famous cogwheel railways of the Jungfrau, the Gornergrat, Pilatus and the two up Rigi, there are other notable examples in Austria (Achensee and Schafberg), in Bavaria (the Zugspitz above Garmisch), and in Savoy (the Montenvers *chemin de fer* to the Mer de glace on Mont Blanc). Nor are they all located in the Alps, as is the case with those on Mt Snowdon in Wales, on the Diakopton–Kalavrita in the Peloponnese, on the hills of Budapest and up to the Nuria monastery in the Catalan Pyrenees. Outside Europe, examples are to be found among the lofty palms of Indonesia, and in the United States the old Mount Washington Railway dates back to 1869, while that of Manitou Pike's Peak, in Colorado, is among the most modern.

Funiculars tend to be associated with certain special places. Apart from specific cases, such as the many Japanese installations serving recreation parks on mountain tops, these tend to be generally concentrated on sea coasts and mountains, in health resorts or in cities.

Among these, therefore, are a number of cliff lifts in British seaside towns, Italy's Marina Grande-Capri, those of Nazaré in Portugal and Monte Igueldo at San Sebastian, and the private lifts installed in the hotels and luxury villas of Acapulco. Funiculars are found in virtually all the famous European spa towns, such as Montecatini, Montreux, Davos, and Baden Baden, etc. – offering pleasant excursions to supplement the cure sessions and visits to the casino.

The city funicular railways often take tourists to the more interesting beauty spots. Examples include the Sacré Coeur in Paris, Mount Lycabettus in Athens and the

The most famous of Swiss high-mountain lines is the Jungfraujoch, rising to a height of 11,330 ft (3,454 m). Three different narrow-gauge, cogwheel railway companies carry an ever increasing number of tourists from Interlaken up to the most famous peak in the Bernese Alps. It is possible to ascend the Jungfrau by two different routes and the line is open even in midwinter, although temperatures sometimes fall to −40°C. The ski centers of Zermatt, Wengen and Mürren, at the express wish of their inhabitants, have banned all forms of motoring and are accessible only on foot or by train.

Opposite: The cars of the amazing cogwheel railway of the Gornergrat climb to an altitude of more than 9,850 ft (3,000 m) in sight of the Matterhorn.

Victoria Peak of Hong Kong, the *elevadores* of Bahia and Lisbon, Mount Carmel in Haifa, Valparaiso in Chile and the one in Wellington, New Zealand.

Paradoxical as it may seem, there are comparatively few in the Alps, perhaps because the cable car is still the quickest way of getting skiers to the top of the piste, even if this spoils the landscape. But the Swiss once again deserve full credit for having recently fostered the astonishing "metro-alpin" systems, dug entirely into the rock of the mountains surrounding Zermatt and Saas-Fee up to a height of almost 11,500 ft (3,500 m), since imitated as well by the French with the "Funival" of the Val d'Isère and its twin of Bourg St Maurice.

Finally there are the cable trams, a pretty rare breed, which run in roadbeds along a semi-enclosed cable, which does not hinder traffic. These enjoyed modest popularity at the beginning of the present century in the hilly districts of Paris and Melbourne, and there is still an interesting example at Llandudno in North Wales (the Great Orme Tramway). But the most celebrated are the cable cars of San Francisco which, after the complete modernization of the century-old installation, were described as the first travelling national monument in the United States and, indeed, the world. The incredible cars which tackle the steep slopes of Russian Hill and Chinatown add much to the charm and special appeal of the city of the Golden Gate.

The journalist Raymond Cartier, a devotee of the concept of technological growth at a time when there was no apparent contradiction between development and progress, was an out-and-out admirer of American society, and California in particular. But he did not understand San Francisco and even less its cable cars. In his essay on the United States, he had this to say about them:

"They existed prior to the 1906 earthquake and have been faithfully rebuilt. Half funicular, half tram, partially open, they are hauled up the steep hill slopes by a steel wire that sings and weeps in its stone groove. At the end of their route, in Market Street, they have to be turned around on small rotating wooden platforms and the passengers obligingly lend a shoulder to help the conductors. Now and then they flatten an automobile and there is always the danger of a cable snapping or of the brakes packing up. The transport companies have offered dozens of times to replace them with buses, even proposing to keep a token line. But San Francisco rebelled. The League for the Defense of the Cable Cars organized a protest. San Francisco was determined to keep its cable cars, every one of them. Until when? The inhabitants boldly replied: "For ever!"

TRAINS OF DREAMS AND REGRETS

The station of Algiers is tucked between the harbour wharves and the hill dominated by the casbah. Nearby, until the mid fifties, the steamers of the Compagnie Transméditerranée, from Ceuta or Marseilles, landed the families of settlers attracted by the mirage of a farm in the Maghreb. Then trains leaving for Constantine, Oran and Béchar would take them to their destination.

Later the paratroops and armoured cars were disembarked there in the desperate attempt to hang on to this most greatly prized colony. The myth of a single France "from Dunkerque to Tamanrasset" was to last a few years more, to the accompaniment of bombs, bullets and brutal

Below: Old funiculars in the Swiss Transport Museum at Lucerne. This system of rail transport is experiencing a revival in many places.

Opposite: Another marvel of Swiss engineering is the very steep cogwheel railway of the Pilatus. The train takes 30 minutes to climb from Alpnachstad, near Lucerne, to the mountain top, from where there is an incomparable view over Lake Lucerne.

In order to improve
the view of the scenery, some Swiss
mountain lines such as the Bernina (below)
and the Monte Generoso cogwheel railway,
provide open cars for tourists in the
summer.
Right: The access ramp from the south to
the Lötschberg Pass, between Brig and
Berne, last of the great first-generation
tunnels, completed just before the outbreak
of the First World War. Today the line,
managed by the private GLS company, is
undergoing improvement, including the
doubling of the stretch running across the
Rhône Valley.

reprisals, until de Gaulle decided to curtail the OAS and grant the territory independence. The Algerians then furiously wiped out all trace of colonial power from the names of streets and towns. Only the railway company still continued for some time to operate under the title Société Nationale des Chemins de fer Algérienne, on the pattern of the SCNF in Paris.

But neither the French nor the Algerians finished one of the boldest rail programmes ever conceived. The Transaharan, departing from the Mediterranean coast and crossing the world's greatest desert, would have linked Algeria with what was then French Equatorial Africa. The prohibitive costs, the hostile presence of Tuareg tribesmen, the process of decolonization and the predominance of long-distance air travel all combined to put an end to this massive undertaking. Today the trains of Algeria travel no farther than Touggourt, 300 miles (500 km) from the coast. The desert has hardly been touched.

The same fate befell the ambitious British imperial dream, devised by Cecil Rhodes, to build one uninterrupted line from the Pyramids to the Cape of Good Hope. Nor was fortune to smile on the idea of a Pan-American rail link from Mexico to Buenos Aires.

Another railroad which remained merely a blueprint was the Hedjaz across the Atlas range which, since the days of the Ottoman Empire, had been intended to reach Mecca, greatly easing the burdens of devout Moslem pilgrims. The legendary Lawrence of Arabia succeeded in blowing up the line that was already there, and the sand did the rest. When, in the 1970s, King Hussein of Jordan revived the plan, he preferred, with less risk, to take the line as far as Aqaba, anticipating, among other things, his Israeli rivals who intended to do

the same in respect of neighbouring Eilat.

There is no saying if the ill-treated mountain pass line, that of Canfranc in the central Pyrenees, which once linked Zaragoza and Toulouse, will be spared. Here, indifference on the part of the French government has contrasted with impassioned support on the Spanish side, notably from *El Pais* which devoted a special issue in its weekly supplement concerning this "muerte de un ferrocarril."

From the bastions of Pau, built by Marshal Vauban, you can see below the station situated on an island in the river which can be reached only by a small funicular, free of charge. Some way off you can see clearly a track that branches from the Gascony line and heads in the direction of the majestic mountains in the distance. Perhaps one day it will be possible to take the train up into the highlands of Aragon and Navarre — a journey that would have pleased even Hemingway.

Left: A guard leans from a car of the legendary Orient Express, the "dream" train now brought back into service and offering its passengers a glamorous journey into the past.

160

One of the small European trains sorely missed by railway aficionados is undoubtedly that of the Val Gardena, in Alto Adige, Italy (South Tyrol), which used to climb more than 3,200 ft (1,000 m) over the twisting 26-mile (42-km) stretch from Chiusa to Plan. The fact that the journey was done by steam engines added a romantic touch. The time required for the trip left something to be desired, but in some circumstances speed is not always a virtue. Nevertheless, where such lines have been preserved and modernized, they are nowadays attracting ever greater numbers of tourists.

On the following pages: A Glacier Express travels along the Albula line in deepest winter.

CHAPTER 6

THE FUTURE OF THE RAILWAYS

164

The train, developed during the early nineteenth century as a powerful engine of the Industrial Revolution, is about to enter a new post-industrial era, as we approach the dawn of a new age. Twenty years ago, few would have had much faith in the survival of the railways; the earliest of the modern forms of transport appeared doomed to irreversible decline.

Given the spread of motoring and the enormous development of civil aviation, there did not seem to be room any longer for the railroad. Yet since then, energy problems and environmental concerns have given a new lease of life to electric traction. The steady growth of cities and the associated shortages of space have given fresh impetus to collective transport. A new generation of fast trains has shown how much more effectively rail, rather than road, can combine speed with safety.

Nevertheless, it would be premature to expect that only good fortune and progress will attend the railways of the future. There remain serious problems, especially taking into account the spoiling tactics of bureaucracy and the inflexibility that still afflicts local and national authorities and which leads to exorbitant running costs, tolerated less and less by governments bent on reducing the level of public expenditure. Furthermore, the likelihood of reversing the trend depends essentially on massive state investment which alone can restore the balance, albeit late in the day, to a transport system which until now has been heavily in favour of the motorized sector.

In assessing future prospects for the countries of Europe, we should bear in mind what is happening in the rest of the world. Thus in North America, the railroads, after touching rock bottom, are now experiencing an unexpected revival; and in countries such as India and China, which have never known the phenomenon of mass-motoring, the train still reigns unrivalled and supreme.

In order to have a balanced perspective of the subject on a global scale, therefore, it seems best to break it down into several broad geographical areas – continents and subcontinents – which present more or less similar features.

Mankind is on the verge of the third millennium of the Christian era while the train is about to enter its third century. Let us hope that its future will be richly rewarding.

EUROPE

The railways only stop when they reach the ocean; at Narvik, on the border with Lapland, at Galway in Ireland, at Brest, forever swept by winds from Brittany, at the little station of Thurso in Scotland, and among the palms of Cascais, at the mouth of the Tagus. Farther south the warm waves of the Mediterranean lap against the trains that stop at Algeciras, facing Morocco, and at Kalamata, at the tip of the Peloponnese.

Despite the post-war prophets who predicted a rapid decline for the railways, despite swingeing cuts made in services in recent years, trains still occupy an important place in the European transport scene. They will take you to the coal-mining suburbs of Charleroi, to Vichy to take the waters or to Santiago di Compostela, following the path of the pilgrims.

Tens of thousands of trains travel the old continental routes every day. In Castile they bear the gaudy insignia of the Spanish Renfe. There are the unmistakable, streamlined, yellow electric trains that speed through the tulip fields of Holland and their red or blue cousins clambering up the Swiss Alps.

Yet a generation has grown up in Europe which to a large extent ignores trains. The development of air traffic, and even more the proliferation of autoroutes, have caused many people to regard the locomotive as an obsolete method of transport. Certainly there are trains which still run to nineteenth-century schedules. Thus a train journey from Athens to Istanbul (there is still a daily train service between the two cities) takes a day and two nights, whereas it is only a couple of hours by air.

Interestingly enough, however, the opposite is also true, and increasingly so,

On the previous page: Tokyo by night. In the Japanese capital 85 per cent of the people use public transport (train, bus or underground railway), an absolute necessity for the efficient functioning and very survival of such a densely populated area. The Japanese Railways (JR) carry about 7,000 million passengers a year, more than all the European rail networks put together.

the TGVs or *trains à grande vitesse* now travel from Paris to the South of France at an average of more than 125 mph (200 km), outdoing both the Air Inter jets and the most speed-crazed motorists. Although the TEEs – which in the 1960s proudly flourished the railway banner – are now consigned to memory, the new conscripts, Intercity and Eurocity, regularly link the main cities of the continent, offering travellers the privileges – which they cannot enjoy in the air or on the road – of restaurant cars, wagons-lits and even nursery areas for the amusement of small children and the relaxation of their parents.

The trains, too, arrive in the heart of the cities, close to all the historic sights and commercial complexes. This explains why the main-line stations in Europe are always bustling with life at any hour of the day or night and are often used as meeting points even for people who never take a train.

The railway revival has been powerfully assisted by the energy problems following the double oil shocks of 1973–79, coupled with the increasing awareness that the car alone cannot solve all transport needs. More recently there has been ecological pressure, whereby the train, by now mostly electrified, has come to be the "green" vehicle *par excellence*, while the automobile conjures up images of noise, acid rain, violence to the countryside and increasingly predictable traffic jams in both summer and winter holiday periods.

It is not surprising, therefore, that there should be more and more talk about the rediscovery of the train, both in its modern context or as speed combined with safety, and in its nostalgic guise whereby it conjures up the fascinating image of its predecessors, evoking the atmosphere and the luxury of bygone times.

It would be a mistake, however, to think

that future prospects for the railways are inevitably rosy; in the long run, everything seems to boil down to the age-old question of profitability. The balance sheets of the exercise – at least for the last couple of decades – have invariably been in the red. This deficit has for the moment become a permanent factor, probably physiological, in the running of the railways in Europe.

In an age dedicated to profit at every level, this means that certain authorities are showing themselves increasingly unsympathetic towards the railways. So from time to time they put forward draconian plans for recovery which entail pruning, as far as possible, lines and services considered, often wrongly, to be secondary, in a vain attempt to put everything on the same level. These are pretended cures which do not take into account the enormous sums that have been allocated and squandered on roads and highways, virtually frustrating any attempt, as things stand, to allow the public and private sec-

tors to compete on equal terms.

On the eve of this second Renaissance, at the very time when most people admit the advantages of rail travel in terms of comfort, safety, saving of energy and care of the environment, European railways must guard against any sudden action by those champions of efficiency who, left to their own devices, would end up by dealing what could be a death blow to a rail network which remains – more than a century after its conception – one of the marvels of human ingenuity.

167

Opposite: The new rolling stock constructed by Fiat Ferroviaria for the Renfe service during a short test run between Turin and Asti (1953).
Below: The marques of the European railway systems.

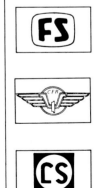

Grand Central Terminal, directly beneath the elegant Pan Am skyscraper, in the heart of New York, was once known as the greatest station in the world. In terms of sheer size, this probably still applies, but certainly not for the number of passengers who mill around daily under its rather gloomy roof, before hurling themselves into the metropolitan inferno. There are more than 40 platforms, on two levels in order to save space in the most valuable urban area in the world, and these have been greatly under-used for many years. Commuter trains depart from here to Connecticut, beside the Adirondack for Montreal, the Maple Leaf for Toronto and the Lake Shore Limited for Chicago.

The Atlantic coast, with its urban galaxy which stretches from Boston to Washington in an almost uninterrupted succession of houses with swimming pools mingling with decaying slums and abandoned industrial plant, is still a railway stronghold. But elsewhere, on the great prairies of the Middle West, in the Rockies and along the Pacific, the passenger train is little more than a toy for high-spending tourists. Union station, Los Angeles, with its elegant colonial architecture, which in its heyday saw glamorous Hollywood actresses and oil tycoons elbowing one another in its waiting rooms, is nowadays comparatively quiet, with only 20 or so trains daily, although these include some famous names, such as The Southwest Chief to Chicago (2,240 miles/3,608 km to the east) and The Coast Starlight to Seattle (1,390 miles/2,237 km to the north). And Dallas, with its very central Transportation Center, only handles The Eagle, the Texan express which pursues its solitary way to San Antonio.

Opposite: A Canadian turbo-train belonging to the national company (CN) during the course of tests made in 1968. This locomotive was then used for the rapid coverage of the Montreal–Toronto route (335 miles/539 km in just over four hours). Passenger traffic in North America is concentrated along the two "corridors" of maximum population density: the Boston–New York–Washington line in the United States and the Quebec–Montreal–Toronto–Windsor line in Canada. Apart from these two itineraries and a few others, such as the stretch between Los Angeles and San Diego, lines are often served by fewer than two trains a day.

Above: The emblem of the Missouri Pacific Railway. Both in the United States and in Canada the private companies tend nowadays to concentrate solely on goods traffic which is more profitable in economic terms.

Many people think, wrongly, that the size of the United States and the resultant expansion of air traffic are the reasons for the eclipse of the railroads. The enormous growth of private motoring, allied with the generous budgets earmarked for highways, explain why Americans have cold-shouldered the railroads. Yet in Europe, where there are just as many cars and equally extensive road networks, such circumstances have not led to the abandonment of trains.

Actually, the decline of the railways in the States is due to a different reason, which has to do with the very essence of the American economic system, based as it is on private enterprise. In the nineteenth century the railroads saw a period of enormous expansion which by 1916 reached a peak in terms of development, with 258,000 miles (416,000 km) of track.

The railroads were then synonymous with profits and unrestrained competition. The lines sprouted like mushrooms, if only to filch clients from rivals only a few miles away or to acquire land. Then came the crash of 1929, the dark years of the Depression and the rise of the motor car. By now it was obvious to everyone that the railways could survive only as a public service and that they could not be run properly without being subsidized.

This was acceptable in Europe, where on 1 January 1947 the British Labour government put the sign "British Railways" on all its trains and stations, following the example of the Germans, the French, and the Italians. The message was not so eagerly received in Washington. Nationalization was the rule, even in Latin American dictatorships, but not in the United States. Ideological trust, against all evidence, in the profit motive proved fatal to train passengers. The companies concentrated all their

168

efforts on goods traffic, still capable of producing dividends, and outdid one another in ridding themselves of inconvenient passengers. Although, for good or ill, federal laws still required certain service obligations, they resorted to all manner of disgraceful stratagems to justify their suppressive actions. Even the carriage windows were no longer cleaned, making it impossible to enjoy the scenery and thus driving away the most devoted clients. Within a few seasons the grandiose main stations, though still crowded, became shadowy barrack-like places frequented by tramps and vandals. So today there is still the spectacle of interminable goods trains trundling slowly along the tracks, which are increasingly liable to be damaged by the heavy loads, while cities with half a million inhabitants, like Nashville and Oklahoma City, have not seen a passenger train go through for years.

Only when the railways seemed threatened by total collapse did the government see fit to intervene. On 1 May 1971 the red and blue stripes of Amtrak appeared on the remaining trains, at least safeguarding the more important connections, such as the transcontinentals and the trains to Florida. But despite the efforts made by the new federal company, still threatened by the curtailment of subsidies which could mean death by suffocation, only the crumbs of interstate traffic returned to rail. In fact, there had to be a strong reason for a traveller to choose a train, because even the journey in a comfortable panoramic car often cost more than the equivalent air fare.

Although the average American traveller still tended to look on the railways as a last resort, trains were nevertheless enjoying a fresh lease of life in the cities. Completely modernized metropolitan lines were operating in San Francisco, Atlanta, Cleveland,

Opposite: General overhaul for a powerful Union Pacific diesel locomotive in the Salt Lake City workshops.
Below: Some Amtrak timetables. This federal company, formed in 1971 to manage passenger services, was the first in American history to stretch from coast to coast, even though its trains run on the lines of private companies which have to grant right of passage. Amtrak recovers 70 per cent of its running costs on fares, an impressive achievement for a passenger service. The trains are often booked weeks in advance.

Washington and Baltimore, often with the all-important support of French or Italian technology, while even the old trolley or tram, in up-to-date, streamlined versions, reappeared in Portland, San Diego, Buffalo and Sacramento: not to mention the "people movers," the futuristic automatic cars which patrolled the center of Miami. This belated victory – even Los Angeles, queen of the automobile, began reconverting to steel and reopened the suburban lines which General Motors had dismantled 30 years earlier to compel Californians to take up motoring – fostered nostalgia, too, for past glories. Many clubs were founded where enthusiasts met each weekend to exchange curios and photographs of the golden age of railways.

171

LATIN AMERICA

In front of the station of Guatemala City stand a couple of soldiers, armed to the teeth. It is not clear whether they are there to protect it, given that the building is used hardly more than three times a week when the small steam trains arrive from Puerto Barrios on the Gulf of Mexico or from Tecun Uman on the Pacific coast. The façade of the modest building has a tablet commemorating the foundation of the Fegua (Ferrocarriles de Guatemala) by President Arbenz during the brief progressive interlude of 1954, before his government was overthrown by the military. The only reform remaining from that distant spell of democracy was the nationalization of the tiny Guatemalan railway network, for by now no landowner is interested in the trains, which are understandably run by the state.

In contrast to Europe and the United States, Latin America has never managed to establish a railway system on a continental scale. South of the Rio Grande the continuity of the Mexican railways is only apparent – there are no direct trains to North American cities – and they come to an end, in any event, at the border with Salvador. Beyond that there is merely a disorganized series of national lines, and often only local lines.

In the countries of Central America, the railway was conceived essentially as a complementary means of carrying goods overland from ocean to ocean. This was the motive behind the Panama–Colón line, the Puntarenas–San José–Limón in Costa Rica and the Corinto–Granada in Nicaragua, where it was even thought worth finding an alternative to the short cross-country journey by using the navigable waters of Lake Nicaragua instead. The

Below: Two Indian women in their characteristic hats board a train run by Enfe, the state company in charge of Bolivian railways. In theory it is possible to travel from Buenos Aires to La Paz, at a height of 13,120 ft (4,000 m), in a couple of days, with a few changes, but entirely by train. The Bolivian network uses the 1-m gauge.

Opposite: A view of the Puno–Cuzco railway line in Peru, crossing the far end of Lake Titicaca, at a height of almost 13,120 ft (4,000 m). From Puno it is possible to continue the journey by hydrofoil or by bus to Guaqui, where the Bolivian rail system begins.

opening of the Panama Canal virtually put paid to all this, so that the trains were reduced to picturesque buses for starving peasants and tourists in search of new adventure.

More or less the same fate befell the railways of Colombia, Ecuador and Peru, the last planned with considerable audacity to cross the Andean range at altitudes that were unthinkable elsewhere. In these cases the trains carried raw materials and agricultural produce to the nearest ports for transshipment abroad, and later they were filled with have-nots attracted by the hypnotic mirage of the great cities.

Only in the "southern cone" of Argentina, Chile and Uruguay is there a network remotely like the European, both with regard to standardization of gauges (only Buenos Aires has three different measures) and the slow decay of plant allowed to rust through lack of investment.

It is no longer possible, though, to cross the continent from the estuary of the Rio della Plata at Valparaiso without boarding a bus between Mendoza, in Argentina, and Santiago. The Chilean trans-Andean lines were closed to passenger traffic perhaps to repay the debt of gratitude owed by Pinochet to the *camioneros* – the bus and truck owners – after the long strike of summer 1973 which dealt the *coup de grâce* to the Allende government. The railwaymen, however, have always been unpopular among the ruling *caudillos*, possibly because they are strongly unionized and solidarity-minded.

Obviously, there are exceptions. If there is still a direct train from Buenos Aires to Asunción (917 miles/1,477 km, two river ferries and 44 hours travel across the monotonous pampas), the credit is probably due to Paraguay's dictator, Alfredo Stroessner, who perhaps deluded himself

that this would somehow reduce the international isolation to which his country had been subjected, for only some ancient trams, reminiscent of the early days of Bavaria, continue to run in the capital.

The basic tendencies of the Latin American economy are very different and do not appear to favour investment in railways. Thus Uruguay has recently suspended the running of passenger trains and large nations such as Venezuela and Brazil are in serious risk of becoming the first to achieve fame by doing without railways altogether.

From Rio Grande do Sur on the Amazon, travel is almost exclusively by air or on buses, while in Venezuela the only line that is functioning is the Barquisimeto–Puerto Caballo, with a diversion to Acarigna, just over 125 miles (200 km) of railway.

Yet there are some encouraging signs of recovery, especially in the big cities, such as Caracas, Rio, San Paolo, Belo Horizonte, Porto Alegre and Recife. Not to mention the ambitions of President Sarney who wants a line of the TGV type which would link the two main cities of Brazil in a couple of hours.

For the time being the only train departing from San Paolo is the Santa Cruz, which has wagon-lit service, and which arrives the following morning at Dom Pedro station in the heart of Rio de Janeiro. Not far from there you can get on to the *bondinho*, the only open tram in the city, and then on the Swiss cogwheel train up the Corcovado to admire one of the most wonderful views in the world, under the outstretched arms of the Christ who once welcomed the immigrants at the end of their ocean crossing and today greets the tourists who have just disembarked from their chartered jet.

THE SOVIET UNION

Many rail services in Europe connect with the Soviet Union. Wagons-lits bound for Moscow can be seen at the Gare du Nord, Paris, at Oslo Sentral, at the legendary Sirkeci station in Istanbul and alongside the dusty platform of Larissa station in the center of Athens. In Asia, they can be found in Teheran, in Pyongyang, Ulan Bator and in Peking (Beijing). They exemplify the grandiose design of a singular railway system which aims to link the Soviet capital with all other countries accessible by rail, without distinguishing between allies and potential adversaries.

Moreover, it is not the railway alone which reflects the wish of the rulers in the Kremlin to promote friendly relations – and this was the case even before the Gorbachev era – given that Aeroflot is by far the most developed airline in the world and that its transatlantic jets are among the few to maintain an air service around the globe. But in the context of railway lines and aircraft hangars, one can detect the ambivalent feelings that govern Russia's contacts with the rest of the world. It is not so much a love-hate relationship as an alternation of fear and admiration where foreigners are concerned, the wish for power and the desire, at the same time, to be accepted and understood.

The tsars built the rail network in the nineteenth century, choosing a gauge bigger than the norm adopted in Europe and China, for fear of military invasions. Thus today the Russian trains can only operate on national territory, as well as in Finland and Mongolia, lands which, prior to the October Revolution, were part of the empire. Then, to overcome the problems caused by this decision, arising as it did from xenophobia, the engineers of the SZD invented a complicated system of trolley exchanges at the frontiers to enable carriages to continue their direct journeys, which still creates heavy additional costs on the transport of Soviet goods. This led to the introduction of wagons-lits with drawn curtains which the Russians, at their own expense, sent halfway across the world, almost as if to affirm their tangible presence.

Clearly the largest nation on earth (with an area of $8^{1}/_{2}$ million sq. miles/22 million km²) still fears isolation, and this must hark back to Stalinist times and the real specter of encirclement. And because of the traditional difficulties associated with maritime transport – all the rivers flowing towards the oceans are paralysed by ice for many months of the year necessitating the passage of "Caudine forks" such as those of the Bosphorus and the Dardanelles – a solution was sought in an enterprise of megalomanic proportions: the Trans-Siberian railway, built with forced labour by deportees at the end of the nineteenth century and recently duplicated, at a prudent distance from the Chinese border.

Tests carried out in 1972 for a high-speed railcar in the USSR were not followed up. Today, however, there is a fast train service between Moscow and Leningrad at over 125 mph (200 kmh). Plans for a high-speed train entail building a new line before the end of the century from Moscow to the Crimea, the Black Sea and the Caucasus, whereby distances of around 1,250 miles (2,000 km) can be covered in a few hours.
Opposite: The emblem of the Soviet Railways (SZD).

Furthermore, Lenin too made his contribution with his journey from Zurich to Petrograd in the "sealed train," through an obliging enemy Germany and neutral Sweden, to Boden, on the frontier with the tsarist empire on the Gulf of Bothnia.

Later the railway became the symbol of the new Soviet society, directed towards heavy industrialization and little inclined, at least until the 1960s, to encourage the development of private motoring. So whereas in 1929 the network of the USSR covered barely 46,000 miles (74,000 km) as against more than 250,000 miles (400,000 km) in the United States, today the situation has been entirely reversed, the former having risen to just over 143,000 miles (230,000 km), the latter having shrunk to 90,000 miles (145,000 km). Soviet superiority is even more pronounced if we compare the traffic data, where the ratio in

the goods transport sector is three to one in its favour, while the gap in the respective passenger services is huge.

Given this fact – and in this field the Russians have overtaken all their rivals – things are not necessarily going all that well with the SZD. The productivity of personnel, as in the case of other state enterprises, leaves much to be desired and from time to time the Kremlin rages against the inefficiency of certain directors, while programmes exist which are designed to reduce the numbers of employees by about 20 per cent. The disappearance of revenue in the small stations lost in the immense spaces of the steppes has been the subject of many reports by Western journalists, and the introduction of speedy services on the Leningrad–Moscow line, deferred from year to year, gives rise to bitter reflections on the frustrated ambitions of those in power. Today, finally, the R200 – a kind of Soviet TGV – covers the 400 miles (650 km) between the two cities in 4 hours 39 minutes. Such a speed has been realized wholly at the expense of the ordinary trains on the route which have to stop at some 13 stations to allow the prestigious express through. And the R200 is a prototype, the only one of its kind, so that it can only do the run once a week, on Thursday from Leningrad and on Friday from Moscow.

Nonetheless, the enormous efforts expended on the railways have produced some results, as outlined. Above all, in the Soviet world, the train is still a means of transport normally used by the ruling class, not only on days devoted to cutting some inaugural ribbon. While Messrs Gorbachev and Shevardnadze appear fully to have adopted the habits of the international diplomatic "jet-set," Brezhnev used to visit his allied capitals in an official train, indifferent to the 30 and more hours

needed to meet Kadar in Budapest or to embrace Dubcek at the little frontier station of Cierna nad Tisou, two days before invading Czechoslovakia.

Opposite: Workers constructing the BAM railway, a new line of more than 1,865 miles (3,000 km) through the harsh territory of eastern Siberia.

Above: The façade of the station at Volgograd (formerly Stalingrad) clearly exhibits the monumental architectural style favoured by the Georgian dictator. The Soviet rail network (SZD) is a colossus in its field. More than half the goods and a quarter of the passengers carried by train throughout the world belong to the USSR.

JAPAN

The commuters line up in Indian file along the yellow rubber stripes on the platforms, opposite the points where the automatic doors of the approaching electric train will open. The train, however, stops a few yards before these marks, so that the passengers can alight in orderly fashion without getting in the way of those waiting to board. Then the empty coaches edge slowly forward to their proper positions and the seats move automatically to face the other direction. There is no standing room on these trains.

At this point the commuters board the train – the platform is on the same level, so they do not need to clamber up – and take their places in the air-conditioned compartment; above their heads the colour television is switched on, providing entertainment during the journey until they reach their stop. Then the train leaves again. The whole procedure has lasted exactly two minutes.

Outside the window the suburbs of Osaka slip by and are eventually replaced by the outlying districts of Kyoto. But the timid student who tries to exchange a few words in English with the foreigners seated next to him, who endeavour to convey to him their admiration for the Japanese transport system, asks innocently: "Why aren't things the same where you come from?"

The fact is that no other nation in the world possesses a railway system comparable to that of the Japanese. The Americans are considerably behind in this field, as are the French, even though they boast the fastest trains anywhere (but the Paris–Lyon TGVs do not leave every six minutes like the Tokyo–Osaka expresses – a metropolitan frequency for a line 342 miles/

552 km in length).

Even the proverbial Swiss punctuality pales before the "bullet trains" of the Shinkansen lines which may deviate from the appointed timetables by not more than 15 seconds. And not even the famous Scandinavian Welfare provides a hostess in the second class who solicitously dispenses water and towels so that the passengers can wash their hands and face. Nor has the impeccable organization in Germany ever thought up a forward baggage system at every station or airport which is so swift, economic and efficient as to allow passengers to travel with almost no encumbrance save the indispensable handbag or briefcase. Busy Victorian London never knew a station like that of Shinjuku in Tokyo (one

of the hundreds in the city), through which, on a normal working day, half a million people pass. Neither in Utrecht nor Groningen does one see such an enormous number of bicycles meticulously lined up in the racks of their owners, who redeem them in the evening, without the need to secure them with an ordinary padlock.

Yet the picture casts some alarming shadows. In fact, the success of the national railways is the outcome of policies wholly directed towards the future economic condition of the empire. Emerging a defeated nation from the Second World War, the Land of the Rising Sun recovered within a few years thanks to an incredible industrial effort which mobilized the energies of the entire population.

The company-family, in fact, demands much but also gives back a great deal. Homes for workers, social security and nurseries for children. All the reconstruction governments up to the 1970s agreed on this policy. In exchange for social peace and quiet and high productivity, they offered almost full employment, low military expenditure and excellent services, notably a network of public transport unrivalled anywhere in the world. In a small, over-populated country, this decision appears perfectly rational.

So during the sixties, while private motoring began to develop, the government, though giving the green light to the construction of highways, did not neglect the railways, building those high-speed lines which represent a leap forward that has altered our very conception of the train.

The state railways came to show a considerable accumulated deficit and every year the figures were substantially in the red. This was mainly due to salary increases and to the burden of making

direct provision to retired personnel (140 pensioners to every 100 still working).

Under these circumstances it was necessary to make drastic staff reductions. The number of railway employees which in 1984 was still 420,000 (having touched 600,000 during the period of cheap manpower) was almost halved within three years, a measure designed to put the company, already broken up into six regional networks, on an even keel in order to facilitate privatization.

Passengers were no happier with the arrangement than the railway personnel, and there was a risk of gradually dwindling services. Some 85 classified secondary lines out of a total of 170 were threatened with closure. Certain stretches near major urban centers were more or less earmarked (as actually happened in some cases) for takeover by private concerns, who were interested in transporting crowds of commuters to and from the gigantic department stores that they ran close to the main-line termini. But who would ransom the *akaji rokaru sen* (the rural lines), such as the Biko line, through the mountains of Hokkaido, the running costs of which by far exceed revenue? Yet these trains constitute a vital link for areas otherwise isolated by snow for many months of the year.

The people thus affected have often taken up cudgels on behalf of the railway workers, while the actions of the Chukakuha extremist group at the end of 1985, ranging from attacks against and occupation of public services, not only paralysed the movement of trains for hours on end but also damaged national productivity in a way that had never happened since the end of the Second World War.

A thorough restructuring of the railway network was probably inevitable, as was the reorganization of manpower resulting from the development of automation. The process, however, was carried beyond reasonable limits, in the pursuit of profit at all costs, to the extent of destroying the social purpose of the services, and the consequences were bound to be considerable, breaking up the tacit pact which had made possible the most impressive economic miracle of our time and would challenge the very legend of Japanese efficiency. The public, inevitably, felt anger and disappointment at this irreversible blow to the system that had been their pride and joy.

INDIA

The crossing of the Iranian desert is a long, arduous journey on overcrowded buses with their scorching daytime temperatures and bitterly cold draughts at night. From Kerman, where the Persian railroads vanish into the sand, to Zahedan, near the Pakistan border, the distance is more than 300 miles (500 km). On the maps we will see the broken line of a railway under construction which is intended to provide the definitive link between the European system and that of the Indian subcontinent. This broken line has been there for decades, originally promised by the father of the late Shah, then by Réza Pahlavi himself and finally by the late Ayatollah Khomeini. Once inside Pakistan, however, we can board the train again, and there is quite a difference between this method of travel and the road route through the Ganges valley.

Perhaps the most tangible legacy of British imperial rule in the land that constituted the "jewel in Her Majesty's crown" was not so much the vaunted constitutional system nor even the English language – which failed to do away with the myriad local dialects – but the railway network. These railroads are the most formidable transport infrastructure ever built by the British in their once extensive empire.

At first the Indian railways remained much like the British ones, with the same type of non-communicating carriages, ticket collectors forced to perform dangerous acrobatics on the footboards of the moving trains, and elegant stations with pedestrian underpasses and old-type signals like those to be found in Kent or Yorkshire. In terms of sheer grandiose architecture, Victoria Terminus, Bombay, far outclassed its eponymous counterpart

*O*n this page and on the following pages: Scenes of trains in India. *Opposite:* A still from the film *A Passage to India.* Indian Railways (IR) maintain a network of over 37,250 miles (60,000 km). Many of the carriages do not have intercommunicating corridors, so that the waiters often have to perform spectacular acrobatic maneuvers on the running boards while the train is moving (see page 183).

in London. This was the case from the Assam, from the Khyber Pass on the Afghan border to Cape Comorin and beyond Adam's Bridge, into Ceylon, to Kandy and Matara. It remains so still, even if the journey from Lahore to Amritsar on the only international train between India and Pakistan, across a Punjab shaken by Sikh secessionism, becomes ever more difficult; and even if the stretch from Rameswaram and Talaimannar, in Sri Lanka, has to be closed every time Tamil terrorism flares up again.

Although mutilated and divided into four states that are often hostile to one another, the Indian rail network is a colossus of hardly imaginable proportions. Indian Railways alone carries some ten million passengers a day, with 11,000 locomotives and 1,600,000 personnel. Despite this top-heavy workforce – unquestionably underpaid by European or American standards – it is a busy, productive organization at a time when public transport is virtually a synonym for unprofitability.

Above all the railway is part of the Indian way of life and the Indian landscape, as perhaps nowhere else in the world. Even in the jet age, the only real way to understand this country is to take the train, just as Gandhi did 70 years ago when, on his return from South Africa, he travelled for months, third class, through Kerala and Uttar Pradesh. The third class still survives, as in all the underdeveloped lands, where social differences are not so pronounced as to have rendered it unacceptable. And we still have those trains with their wonderfully evocative names – Radjhani Express, Taj Express, Frontier Mail and Deccan Queen.

Throughout the modern history of the subcontinent the railways have featured prominently in major social dramas and upheavals – the massacre of entire coachloads of Hindu and Muslim refugees in 1948, the flight of tattered hordes of Bengalis in 1971 which delivered the *coup de grâce* to an already desperate Calcutta, and the stationmaster of Bophal who, before dying of poisoning, managed to clear the way for a train full of passengers which had stopped in the station on the evening of the Union Carbide disaster. Whether this was an act of heroism or merely the obligation to adhere to the timetable, we shall never know.

The timetable itself was another legacy of the British. Although there are no precise statistics, and in spite of insurrections, floods and accidents of all kinds which are likely to have unpredictable effects on any given journey, there is still a greater likelihood of arriving on time in India than in

many far more highly developed countries.

Although cows often nibble at the blades of grass on the platforms and the railway employees scribble away at their papers by candlelight, passengers regularly welcome the sight of their train pulling in at exactly the moment it is due. It is an incredible mixture of utter unpredictability and extreme organization, and it is astonishing, in the circumstances, that it all works so well.

For years Bengal has been shaken by bloody insurrection, yet the trains have continued to arrive at the huge station of Howrah, in the heart of the most poverty-stricken quarter of Calcutta, rumbling over the Hoogly iron bridge, pride of British engineering and today crossed by millions of people who live and work in the over-crowded city.

Perhaps this success can be explained by the relationship of the population and the railways. Although the train was introduced by Europeans and represented the most enormous achievement in moderniz-ing the lives of the rural masses – along with the cinema, which is nowhere more pop-ular than in India – people have never dis-played any hostility to the steam engine. In a society permeated with a sense of holiness and magic, the railway was at first accepted and later assimilated without any profound adverse effects on local customs and beliefs. Therefore the station has become the mirror of Hindu village life, where people eat, sleep, laugh and sometimes die alongside those awaiting the train. And the symbol of European dominance, having been taken over by the former subjects, still continues to be one of the most power-ful defenses against the dissolution of an immense country.

CHINA

Opposite the skyscrapers that crown the island of Victoria giving it the appearance of a second Manhattan, in the center of the bay of Hong Kong, rises the clocktower of the Kowloon–Canton Railway. During the 1960s this was the departure point for the exploration of the vast land beyond the so-called Bamboo Curtain, an experience reserved for only a few privileged tourists at a time when Mao was urging millions of inhabitants of the most highly populated nation on earth to rely on their own re-sources and not to admit the contamination of foreign influences.

The station of Hong Kong, nowadays greatly modernized, is still an excellent point of departure for the People's Repub-lic, even though crowds of tourists now fly directly to Peking. But since airlines are so heavily booked, many inland journeys are best accomplished by rail, offering the dis-cerning visitor a glimpse of Chinese society that is much more vivid and real than the necessarily stereotyped images conveyed by local guides.

In fact, the train is the principal way of getting to know this immense country, where private motoring is still rudiment-ary, despite the eager expectations of Euro-pean and Japanese firms which long to get a foothold in a market of this size. Yet the development of the railways was no simple undertaking in the dying days of the Man-chu Empire, pervaded by decadence, cor-ruption and hysterical xenophobia. When the first line was opened between Shanghai and Woosung in 1876 (a year when Euro-peans were already travelling regularly by train), Confucian traditionalists were firmly opposed to the steam engine, deemed guilty, in its passage through the country-side, of disturbing the souls of the dead.

"LOWU" MAIN GATE OF SINO–BRITISH BORDER

Thus, what with palace intrigues, peasant uprisings, bloody civil wars and foreign occupations, by 1962, three years after the final victory of the Red Army over the troops of Chiang Kai-shek, barely 17,400 miles (28,000 km) of track had been laid in China, mainly near the coasts and across the plains of Manchuria, heart of the industrial region built up by the Japanese. But thanks to the decisiveness of the new regime, the development of the lines has literally doubled in the meantime – today it spans 33,850 miles (54,500 km) – a rate of growth unthinkable elsewhere. The speed of the trains has noticeably increased (during the same period the time for the journey from Peking to Shanghai was halved, from 26 to 13 hours), even though the electric trains running on the nationalist island of Taiwan have likewise become faster and more frequent.

But this rapid development has not managed to keep step with the economic expansion that recently took place during the reforming period of Deng Xiao Ping; and if the infrastructures do not quickly prove equal to the demand, the transport system – of passengers and, above all, of goods – may well come under threat.

In the last few decades the Chinese railways have felt the dire effects of excessive autarchy. Electrification has not been encouraged, for example, and steam engines have continued to be built, given the quantity of coal which the mines are able to produce. Staff levels have increased enormously over the years and more than three million employees of the Chinese railways have made it the largest company on earth, at least in terms of numbers. Having said that, however, only a part of this vast army is involved in the actual movement of the trains, while the national railways perform numerous other tasks of a

Below: A Chinese-made steam locomotive being unloaded in the Japanese port of Yokohama for an exhibition. China is the last nation in the world that still manufactures steam engines.
Opposite: A train on the new Anhui–Jiangxi line, built in the early eighties, along a stretch of 342 miles (551 km).
Opposite above: The bridge of Lo Wu, marking the border between the Chinese People's Republic and the British colony of Hong Kong which will be returned to China in 1997.

type unknown elsewhere. It is not by chance that in China there is an Academy of Railway Sciences, responsible, among other things, for the training of personnel. The future of the railways in the centuries to come will depend to a large extent on the successful endeavours of this organization.

The challenge is not only quantitative but also geographical, in that it has to unite the country by linking the innermost and least hospitable zones. The railways have been extended in Sinkiang beyond Urumqui towards the Islamic provinces of central Asia and the USSR, along the ancient Silk Road and, in the other direction, work has already begun on the line that will reach Lhasa, at a height of 13,100 ft (4,000 m) – the roof of the world.

This Tibetan venture, reminiscent of the heroic early days of the railways, is being carried out in a land where the winter lasts six months and where snow still falls in June, and where no rain falls in summer

and sandstorms rage at 50 mph (80 kmh). Certainly, when passengers are able to alight at the foot of the imposing Potala, the palace which once belonged to the Dalai Lama, the railway will have marked up yet another milestone in its amazing history.

*B*elow: A train used for plantation work on the small island of Nossi Bé, off Madagascar. Lines such as these, often on the "Decauville" gauge, are found mainly in Cuba for the transport of sugar cane. Other unusual lines for use on farms or in mines are found in remote areas, e.g. the Fiji archipelago and Australian-owned Christmas Island, south of Java.
Opposite below: Colonial echoes at the small station of Sidi Bou Said in Tunisia; *above:* The artist Paul Klee during a trip to Tunisia in 1914. Klee travelled by train to Sidi Bou Said and Carthage.

186

AFRICA

Anyone disembarking at Goulette, the port of Tunis, permanently clogged with traffic, will immediately find efficient electric trains shuttling to and from the capital. The city also boasts ultra-modern green trams, a transport system launched a few years back.

But Africa, of course, is not all like this. Between the Mediterranean and the southernmost lands, there is an enormous central region, along the track where the mythical Cairo to Cape line was to have run, which is the setting for the most absurd and picturesque trains in the world. You can begin the journey from Alexandria, from the small suburban station of Aboukir, famous for the naval battle which was the first encounter between Nelson and Napoleon. And at once it is evident that in Egypt, as in the rest of black Africa, people huddle in clusters on the carriage roofs. The journey is interrupted at Sadd El Ali – the great dam just after Aswan – to take a two-day trip on Lake Nasser to Wadi Halfa in Sudan. Assuming you survive the torrid desert heat of the Nubian desert, you will eventually reach Khartoum and then, with a government pass, Waw, 870 miles (1,400 km) farther south. After that comes the virgin equatorial forest and frontiers ever more impenetrable by reason of the luxuriant vegetation.

The spread of air traffic and the feuds between governments have combined to make an overland journey through Africa extremely difficult and tiring. Where there are not rebels threatening the tracks, as often happens on the Djibouti–Addis Ababa line, there are dictators intent upon impeding international traffic in reprisal for some slight. Until the mid seventies the countries of the former British East African empire – Uganda, Kenya and Tanzania – operated only one railway company in common. Then the direct trains from Mombasa to Kampala and from Nairobi to Dar Es Salaam were relegated to the memory of the bygone days of Karen Blixen.

The same fate attended southern Africa, the only part of the continent equipped with a homogeneous network of the 1-067 mm Cape gauge. With the crumbling of the Portuguese colonial empire and the subsequent guerrilla warfare between the Marxist governments of Angola and Mozambique and the mercenaries and invading forces of South Africa, there was no longer any possibility of travelling from Luanda to Maputo, or from one ocean to the other, through five states. And for

every frontier which reopened, as the one at Livingstone between Zambia and Zimbabwe, many others became impracticable.

But Africa continues to look on the future of the railways with confidence. Although the prospect of unification, dear to colonialist interests, has vanished, the importance of the train in the context of nationalism has correspondingly increased. Thus King Hassan of Morocco is in favour of a line beyond Marrakesh to consolidate his own power in those territories threatened by the Polisario, and a regular service between Casablanca and Rabat has been introduced which could be the envy of any European line. The progressive rulers of Burkina Faso (formerly Upper Volta) are fighting their battle on

behalf of rail against the Sahel Desert and against the World Bank – which has turned down every financial appeal for new railways in the Third World – to carry the line beyond Ouagadougou to Tanmbao on the border with Mali.

It is a tough and brave undertaking for an extremely poor country which can take comfort in the successes already recorded in Cameroon and Gabon, where President Omar Bongo provided solid support to the mammoth task of cutting the Transgabonese line for 415 miles (670 km) through the jungle. When the second part of the line was opened to Natal in 1986, French premier Jacques Chirac travelled in the first train of honour.

AUSTRALIA

The place has an exotic name but only old-timers can appreciate its true meaning. The boundless Nullabor Plain, where there is scarcely a speck of greenery, is crossed by a railway which boasts the longest straight stretch of line in the world, almost 310 miles (500 km) without the merest hint of a curve. The so-called Tea and Sugar Train stops at all the small stations on the way and each time a small crowd, made up of descendants of the pioneers who built the railway, gather round the train to stock up with supplies of food, clothing, toys and, of course, beer.

Fifteen million people live in this continent of immense distances and, for many, deep solitude. What can be the purpose, then, of the train in a country where even the doctor runs his own private plane to reach isolated communities, sometimes consisting only of a single family? Yet bookings for the most famous expresses such as the Southern Aurora and the Sunlander have to be made months in advance, and the glossy publicity brochures of the National Tourist Board declare, with a measure of pride, that Australian trains represent the dream of railway enthusiasts the world over, who are prepared to save up for years, if need be, to treat themselves to a trip on the Indian Pacific.

The Australian railways serve mainly the east coast and operate numerous branch lines in the states of Victoria and New South Wales, where British colonization was concentrated in the nineteenth century. The network, consisting of more than 25,000 miles (40,000 km) of track, spans the entire continent, to the port of Fremantle, near Perth, on the Indian Ocean, and to Cairns, facing the Pacific Barrier Reef, 4,130 miles (6,650 km) away.

In spite of the different administrations (every state has its own company) and gauges (broad in Victoria, narrow in Queensland, standard elsewhere), and despite the prevalence of private motoring and air travel, the trains carry more than 400 million passengers a year. These figures, however, are slightly deceptive, for the majority of users are commuters who take advantage of the excellent services around Sydney, Melbourne, Brisbane, Adelaide and Perth.

Yet even over medium and long distances the condition of Australian trains is considerably more healthy than that of their United States counterparts. In particular, the eastern regions are provided with local services – which have vanished in America – that carry passengers from the coastal cities to the outback. Some of these lines are served by high-speed turbine locomotives, the XPTs. This is a clear sign that it was the decision to defend privatization at all costs which led to the collapse of the passenger services on the American railroads.

Australia, on the other hand, although wedded to a market economy, is less rigid and selective. The wide open spaces and the considerable wealth help to ensure that competition is not protracted outside office hours. In neighbouring New Zealand the working week has now been reduced to barely four days. There is ample time, therefore, for hobbies, ranging from tennis to sailing and surfing; and also train trips. You can take along the car on the Motorrail Express to the beaches of the Gold Coast, or travel on the electric train to the New Zealand Alps and Arthur's Pass, with Swiss-style scenery.

Our long journey on the world's railways may appropriately end, therefore, at the terminal of Perth, facing one of the

Below: The little station of Kuranda, surrounded by tropical vegetation, in northern Queensland. Situated along the line which links the port of Cairns to Forsayth, it is served by a very popular tourist train.
Opposite: A hotel built by the East Africa Railway which until the 1970s ran the railway networks in Kenya, Uganda and Tanzania.

loveliest and cleanest bays anywhere in the world, or on one of the restaurant trams – with windows discreetly shaded and *fin de siècle* lamps – where you can enjoy dinner or afternoon tea on the broad streets of Melbourne. Or on the tiny station platform of Kuranda, buried among the tropical bougainvilleas in the forest of northern Queensland. There is no doubt that everyone should come here, at least once in a lifetime.

PICTURE SOURCES

Ermanno Albertelli Editore, 79; 80; 81.
— **A.F.E.** (Archivio Fotografico Enciclope-dico), 66; 67 (Angelo Pennoni); 68; 70; 72-73 (Angelo Novi); 78; 83; 181; 129. — **Paolo Baggio, Anna Topan,** 186; — **Archivio Enrico Castruccio,** 61: 168. — **Alberto Conforti,** 60; 86; 113; 123 (below); 165; 178; 179 (center); 187.
— **Anne Conway,** 4; 32; 142; 143.
— **Deutsche Bundesbahn,** 42; 43; 148. — **Massimo Ferrari,** 88. — **Ferrovie Nord Milano,** 13; 30; 39; 51; 52 (Cesare Colombo); 59 (Cesare Colombo); 139 (Cesare Colombo); 144; 152 (Cesare Colombo); 190 (Cesare Colombo). — **Fs** (Ferrovie dello Stato), 2-3; 5; 18; 48; 76; 102; 105; 106. — **Philip J. Griffiths**/Magnum, 147.
— **Erich Hartmann** Magnum, 98. **LL-Viollet,** 55 (below). — **Steve McCurry**/Magnum, 180; 182; 183. — **Orient Express Turismo,** 24; 25; 28; 29; 49; 91; 160. — **Antonio Pisacreta,** 84; 85. — **Press Tours,** 109; 110; 111. — **Publifoto,** 11; 14; 22; 27; 34; 38; 44; 45; 47; 54; 69; 75; 82; 89; 93; 103; 104; 120; 122; 137; 140; 149; 161; 166; 169; 170; 175; 176; 184 (large photograph); 185. — **Simone Sabbieti,** 112; 171. — **Stefano Scatà,** 126; 127 (left); 131; 173. **R. Singh**/Ana, 116; 117.
— **Studio Aulenti,** 56; 57. — **Swiss National Tourist Board,** 21; 100; 101; 135; 141; 154; 155; 156; 156; 157; 157; 158; 159; 162-163. — **Patrick Ward**/Ana, 94; 95. — **P. Zachmann**/Magnum, 9.

SELECT BIBLIOGRAPHY

Benji, Pascal *Les Chemins de Fer de la Corse* (La Régordane)

Caminada, Paul *Der Glacier Express* (Desertina Verlag)

Carper, Robert S. *American Railroad in Transition* (Barnes)

Fistell, Ira *America by Train* (Burt Franklin and Co.)

Hirota, Naotaka *The Lure of Japan's Railways* (Japan Times)

Lamplugh, Barbara *Transiberia by Rail* (Lascelles)

Pifferi, Enzo *Ande: Le ferrovie piú alte della Terra* (Silvana Editoriale)

Pet, Paul Inde: *Paradis des Trains* (Payot)

Riboud, Marc *Gares et Trains* (Ace Editeur)

Amin, Willets and Matheson *Railway across the Equator* (The Bodley Head)

Les temps des gares (Exhibition catalogue, Pompidou Center, Paris)

Europa Eisenbahn Atlas (Kümmerly & Frei)

S- und U-bahnarchitektur in Berlin (Felgentrett & Goebel)